SILKY TERRIERS
TODAY

Hingeley, Marshall & Wren

Howell Book House

New York

HOWELL BOOK HOUSE
A Simon & Schuster / Macmillan Company
1633 Broadway
New York, NY 10019

MACMILLAN is a registered trademark of Macmillan, Inc.

Library of Congress Cataloging-in-Publication data
available on request.

ISBN 0–87605–325–8

Manufactured in Singapore

10 9 8 7 6 5 4 3 2 1

Contents

We dedicate this book
to all our past Australian Silky Terriers
who have helped make this wonderful
little dog of today, and tomorrow.

A*CKNOWLEDGEMENTS*

We are extremely grateful to all those friends who have generously helped us in gathering information for this book. It would be impossible to say 'thank you' to all, but there must be a special mention for Mrs Elaine Anderson, Betty and Phyl Reid, Dayna Scales, Michaela Hunt, Anne Crenfelot (NZ), Dave White and special thanks to Mark Burns.

Thanks are also due to Sheridan Pausey, for her contribution on Caesarean sections, to Viv Rainsbury for her excellent line drawings, and to all those who sent photographs of their dogs.

*Photo: Russell
Fine Art.*

*I*NTRODUCTION

It is perhaps surprising that a breed which has, essentially, been developed from the raw materials of a cocktail of British breeds should have taken so long to achieve any degree of popularity in the British Isles. However, despite the fact that the breed is still not accorded Challenge Certificate status by the Kennel Club, it steadily attracts new admirers.

While the evolution of the Silky is shrouded in a degree of mystery, largely due to the fact that accurate records of its early development were not chronicled, there can be little doubt that, when the Australian continent was being settled, British migrants took with them a selection of early British terrier types, several of which were instrumental in developing the Silky, and its other indigenous cousin, the Australian Terrier. Writers have previously suggested that primitive Skye, Dandie Dinmont, Norwich, Border and Cairn Terriers were the forefathers of the breed, as well as the toy Yorkshire Terrier and other minor Terrier breeds now extinct, such as the Clydesdale, or the Paisley Terrier, which was known for its straight, silky coat.

At a time when selective breeding was in its infancy and marked type differentials were much less acute than they are today, many of these early terriers were considerably more alike than they are now. Certainly a photograph of a Scottish Terrier named Wolden Scottish Wonder, which appeared in *The Dog in Australia* in 1897, bears little similarity to the breed as we know it today, and yet is remarkably like the Rough Coated Terrier depicted in the same publication. I doubt whether there will ever be total agreement as to how the breed exactly developed, but develop it did, until such time as the Australian Silky Terrier, despite having survived several name changes during its short history, became a popular exhibition and companion dog in Australia and, subsequently, in the USA and other countries.

In truth, its original popularity, once established, must be down to the fact that a convenient-sized dog, with instant companion appeal, which also had the determination of Terrier characteristics, with an in-built prowess for keeping vermin and snakes at bay, would have had instant appeal to the early Australian urban dwellers. The Silky is aesthetically more of a

*The Australian
Silky Terrier is a
breed with instant
companion appeal.*

glamorous pet than the Australian Terrier and yet appears more robust and substantial than the ever-refined Yorkshire, whose grooming demands may put off the more faint-hearted of owners.

Perhaps one of the main reasons for the Silky's slow progress in the companion dog charts in Great Britain has been the fact that the Yorkshire has, for many generations, held great sway with the general public. Furthermore, Yorkies which are not bred with the show ring in mind, so a strict regime of line-breeding is not a priority, tend to be larger and heavier than their exhibition-oriented cousins. The fact that so many Yorkies which appear in the pet marketplace seem, to the uninitiated, to look rather like Silkies has made it more difficult for the Silky to sell itself on the grounds of any great uniqueness. Any expert will tell you that there are several marked differences between the Australian, the Silky and the Yorkie, but such differences are perhaps too subtle to be apparent to the layman and are, therefore, of little relevance.

In the United States, the breed's initial popularity owes much to the publication *This Week*, a widely read magazine of the period which elected to feature a Silky puppy on the front cover of its edition of November 28th 1954. This tousled character, Redway Boy Blue by name, was the ultimate in "cute", and as soon as his cheeky face hit the streets, the publication was inundated with enquiries as to where readers could obtain one of these – at the time – extremely rare dogs. Several personalities in the public eye elected to have a Silky as a companion and very soon the breed became known by the general public. Such exposure has never been afforded to the breed in Britain, but looking on the positive side, this has meant that the Silky has never been exploited or commercialised in the UK. Nonetheless, it remains an uphill struggle for the breed to rid itself of the "bad Yorkie" image. Silky

Terriers were first imported into Britain as early as the 1930s, and the breed was featured (as the Sydney Silky) in the famed *Hutchinson's Dog Encyclopaedia*. It was not until almost half a century later that the inaugural meeting of the British breed club was held and, to this day, the Silky remains in the hands of a few dedicated fanciers.

The breed's obvious virtues, both physical and mental, are well known to all who associate with it. With the help of this book, written by specialists, all of whom have intimate knowledge of the breed, the charms of the Silky will, hopefully, be apparent to a much wider readership of dog lovers who want to share their life with a glamorous yet sturdy Toy dog who is also a real Terrier at heart.

ANDREW H. BRACE

1 HISTORY OF THE SILKY TERRIER

This is a real Australian, the first and only Toy originating in Australia. The Australian Silky Terrier is both a hardy and a fun-loving little dog, low-set, with a strong terrier character in alertness, activity and soundness. Australian Silkies make smart show dogs and, with their love of exercise and will to work, can kill a rat in seconds and have been known to kill snakes. For children and elderly people they are a great asset in the playground or home, they are an admirable deterrent for uninvited visitors and they give wonderful companionship. These great little dogs would die for you if need be.

BACKGROUND TO THE SILKY

When English settlers arrived in mainland Australia and Tasmania during the mid-19th century, they brought not only their personal goods, but many brought their pets. Among the animals were terriers, and the fittest of the terriers survived in this new country: they were known as Broken

Cairn Terriers: One of the breeds which could have influenced the development of the Australian Terrier.

Reproduced from Hutchinson's Dog Encyclopaedia

Coated Terriers and Waterside Terriers. Before discussing the origin of the Australian Silky Terrier, we should look at the origin of the Australian Terrier and the Yorkshire Terrier.

ORIGIN OF THE AUSTRALIAN TERRIER

It is almost certain that the Australian Terrier descended from the Broken Coated Terriers of Tasmania around the middle of the last century. No records were kept on the early breeding of the Australian Terrier, but it was most likely the result of crossing the Broken Coated Terrier, the Dandie Dinmont, the Skye Terrier and a Scotch Terrier (not to be confused with the Scottish Terriers). This opinion was shared by a Queensland judge, the late Fred David. Fred David also described the Scotch Terrier as a rough-coated varmint of a dog, black-and-tan or even ginger red in colour.

The Australian Terrier got his silky hair top-knot from the Dandie Dinmont, and the body length from the Skye; from time to time the Manchester Terrier was used to improve the rich tan colour, and some say the Cairn Terrier was also introduced. While blue and tan predominate in the breed, some nice reds are seen today. The Australian Terrier is one of the smallest working terriers, standing just 25cms or 9.75 ins and weighing a mere 6.6 kilos, or 14.5 lbs. The dogs were used as guard dogs in the Australian outback farms and in mines, and for looking after flocks of sheep, where their keen eye-sight and hearing helped them give early warning of danger. Their natural fierceness was sufficient to deter anything but the boldest predator. Just like the Australian Silky Terrier, the Australian Terrier would die for you if need be.

ORIGIN AND BACKGROUND OF THE YORKSHIRE TERRIER

In early days a Mrs M.A. Foster of Bradford in England had a top-winning dog, Bradford Hero: the dog had won 100 first prizes. This dog's pedigree included all the top dogs over the previous 35 years. They were all Scotch Terriers. The name Yorkshire was given to them because the breeding was improved in Bradford, a city in the county of Yorkshire. A few years later a Mr C. Boatman of Halifax wrote an article on the breed for a journal called *TheEnglish Stock Keeper*. He was writing about Swift's Old Crab, a cross-bred Scotch terrier, who had been mated to Kershaw's Kitty, a Skye, and an old English Terrier bitch owned by a Mr Whittam of Halifax. The owner of Old Crab also resided in Halifax; he was a carpenter by trade. Later Old Crab's owner moved to Manchester and from there he sent Old Crab back to Halifax to visit Kitty. The last mating was about 1851. Coincidentally, Kershaw and Whittam were both publicans. Old Crab was described as being of about eight to nine pounds with a good terrier head and eye, although too long in body, but with good tan on his legs and muzzle, and with a coat about three to four inches long. Kershaw's Kitty, who was part Skye and part Black-and-Tan English Terrier had, prior to 1851, six litters, all by Old Crab – thirty-six puppies in all, twenty-eight males and eight females. Kershaw's Kitty had drop ears and plenty of coat. Neither the dog nor the bitch had a pedigree. After 1851 this little bitch was stolen and then came into the possession of a Mr Jagger. Kitty then had forty-four more puppies, making a total of eighty.

Then there was an old English Terrier bitch kept by Mr Whittam. She had good tan colour, head, ears, legs and a short grizzle, but she was built for speed and also had no pedigree. We have no name for this bitch but she was first owned by a Bernard Hartley of Allen Gate in Halifax.

Let us go over the description of these dogs. Old Crab, with a terrier head, three-quarters inches of coat, a long body and tan, was most like a Clydesdale or Waterside Terrier. Kitty, with plenty of coat and a good blue coat but no tan, no doubt a Paisley terrier, and Mr Whittam's bitch (with no name) built for speed, tan head and legs and a short grizzle back. Certainly she was out of an Old English terrier. The dogs were shown under Broken Haired Scotch Terriers. In the 1870s Angus Sutherland of Accrington, a reporter for *The Field* reported that they should no longer be called Scotch terriers but Yorkshire Terriers. So Kitty, Old Crab, and Mr Whittam's bitch of no name produced the pattern for the Yorkshire Terrier and, along with the Australian Terrier, laid out the blueprint for the Australian Silky Terrier.

THE ORIGIN OF THE AUSTRALIAN SILKY

Many of our older breeders believe that the Australian Silky was, most likely, the result of mating the Australian Terrier to a Yorkshire Terrier. But let us go back to the 1820s. It is known that Mr Scott of Ross, in Tasmania, successfully bred Broken-Coated Terriers with good blue body coats. It is also known that the Broken-Coated Terriers, also known as Waterside Terriers, had arrived with free settlers to mainland Australia and Tasmania from Scotland. In the late 1820s two Broken Coated Terriers, male and female, were taken back to England from Tasmania; unfortunately the

male died on the voyage. The female survived the crossing, and was later mated to a Dandie Dinmont Terrier. She had several litters to this dog. The puppies were very alert and active, with good blue coats.

Macarthur Little, an early Australian settler from London, was so impressed by their type and temperament that he purchased several of the puppies. He then set about a breeding pattern to produce a small terrier with a soft and longer coat, using the Yorkshire Terrier as an outcross. In 1862 Macarthur Little arrived in Australia, and after settling at Pennant Hills just outside of Parramatta, he continued to breed this small terrier. To add more size to the dog, Little used a rough terrier, also known as a Broken Haired or Wire Haired Terrier, but by the 1890s this breed had become known as the Australian Terrier.

Charles Hinchcliffe acquired several puppies from Macarthur Little, and took them back to the goldfields in Ballarat, Victoria. The Silky Coated Terriers were very popular, and a few kennels were set up in Victoria and South Australia. The notes of one older breeder, Anne Richardson (Valanne Kennels), reveal that a Silky was shown in 1880, when a 'Broken Coated Blue and Tan Terrier, Under 7lbs.' was exhibited at a Sydney Show. Later they were described as Rough Coated Blue Terriers, Blue and Tan or Soft or Silky Haired Terriers. In the 1901 Sydney Royal Show the breed was classified for the first time. Only two entered: Mr Matterson's dog Silvermine, bred in Tasmania by Mr E. Richie, won first over Mr G. Smith's Dollie. The next year Silvermine was shown under the title of Champion. One of his puppies was shown as a 'Terrier Australian, Rough Coated Any Colour, Under 8 lbs.'

It is difficult to ascertain just when the

The Yorkshire Terrier was imported to Australia, and was highly influential in the development of the Australian Silky Terrier.

first Yorkshire Terrier arrived in Australia, but apparently, in 1872, a Mr J. Spink had exported a male named Punch, a grandson of Old Sandy from a Halifax bitch, to a Norman D'Arcy of Brisbane, Queensland. Before leaving England, Punch had won prizes at 13 shows. The breed was not popular in the Colonies, according to Walter Beilby in his book *The Dogs of Australia*, 1897. However, many exhibits were sired by Yorkshire Terriers. A Mr R. Copeland showed his bitch Dandy IXL as a Terrier Sydney Silky in the open bitch class, and another bitch, Dandy Mattie, in the Terrier Yorkshire open class. Both bitches were out of the same bitch, the imported English Yorkie, Tiney. This bitch had been mated to a registered Sydney Silky, Nip of Toohey. It was not until the 1930s that it was prohibited to outcross with Yorkshire Terriers, when breeders agreed they were losing the terrier character, and puppies were getting too small.

In *The Dogs of Australia* 1897, there is no mention of the Silky. But in *Tysack's Annual*, C.S. Turner wrote the following in 1912.

"Its sire was Australian; component parts were many –
Yorkshire, Black and Tan and Scotch – it proved much worse than any.
Another dash of Yorkshire; result was far more pretty;
They called it Sydney Silky, but quarrel over the city."

There is no doubt Silkies were being shown at the end of the last century.

DEVELOPMENT OF THE AUSTRALIAN SILKY

The first State to recognise the Silky was Victoria, and probably the first mention of the Silky Terrier being a specific breed of Australian Terrier was in the *Weekly Time Kennel* notes published on April 1st 1905. In this column there was talk of the Victorian Australian Terrier Club having functioned for four years, and as having the Silky specimen excluded from the Standard for the Australian Terrier. This exclusion was not adhered to, as many varied types and coat textures were still shown together.

In 1906 classes for Silky Coated Terriers

ABOVE: A Sydney Silky: One of the early examples of the breed that was to become known as the Australian Silky Terrier.

BELOW: Aust. Ch. Ensta Fancy Freeby: The Australian Silky Terrier now has a following worldwide.

began to appear at a lot of shows. In 1908 the newly-formed Victorian Silky and Yorkshire Terrier Club applied for separate classes for Silky Terriers at shows, but the controlling body of the day refused the request. The Victorian Silky and Yorkshire Terrier club again applied for separate classes for Silky Terriers at the upcoming show of the Victorian Poultry and Kennel Club, but the request was again declined. A separate classification for Silky Terriers was first provided at the Victorian Poultry and Kennel Club held from June 7th to June 10th 1911.

The first Club formed in New South Wales was in 1906. Sydney breeders decided to have their own Standard, and the breed became known as The Sydney Silky (the name Sydney Silky is still sometimes used today and one well-known breeder, Mrs R. Greer, was very disappointed at any name change). According to the New South Wales

Standard, ears were to be pointed and clean of long hair – which is still a must today. Weight was to be a maximum of twelve pounds or a minimum of six pounds. *Tysack's Annual* 1912 stated that Australian Terriers with longer coats were called Australian Silky Terriers, and that judges were called upon to certify whether each specimen was an Australian Terrier, a Silky Terrier or a Yorkshire Terrier. The breed was going downhill fast. Many dogs were more like Yorkshire Terriers weighing only three to four pounds – much too small to breed, and not sound, and many bitches were lost in whelping because of their size. Judges would not award challenges to these tiny dogs.

The breed progressed with large numbers of tiny dogs, with the hope of them taking the place of the Yorkshire Terrier in Victoria. In 1932 the Victorian Controlling Body, now the Kennel Control Council, were forced to take action about this state of affairs, and in 1934 it prohibited the inter-breeding and registration of crosses between Yorkshire Terriers and Silky Terriers. In July 1958 twenty-seven dogs were weighed and measured; eight pounds six ounces was the average weight, with nine-and-three-quarters to ten inches in height at the withers, a body length of twelve inches and a coat of five to six inches. At the 1959 Royal Show, Mr Frank Longmore (Victoria) met with New South Wales Kennel Control. The new Standard was approved and adopted by both States. At last breeders agreed to the new Standard. The breed was to be known as The Australian Silky Terrier.

Silky breeders have progressed so far today. It has been a long hard road, all uphill, but now that they have succeeded in reaching the top with their breeding, they are concerned that it should not go backward. More and more breeders are planning together, and this is the only way to go. Today, they have not only a few top Australian Silkies, but they claim to have the best in the world, and that is how it should be. The late G. Holmes once said: "Judges should look for an Australian Silky that shows life and vitality in sound, free action, that stands in the centre of the ring, head up, ears and tail erect and that looks the Judge in the eye and asks for it." Today's Australian Silkies are doing just that.

INTRODUCTION TO AMERICA

The Australian Silky Terrier has gone through many changes since the breed's introduction into the United States in the early 1930s, when early Silkies were imported into the US from their country of origin, Australia. The first imports to be recorded were in the late 1940s. Their title has changed from the Sidney Silky Terrier, or Australian Silky Terrier, to the name currently used in America, the Silky Terrier. By 1955 Silkies were being entered in shows throughout the US and a concentrated group aimed to popularise them. On July 4th 1959 Silky Terriers became the 113th breed eligible to compete for Championship points and, by the end of that year, eight Silkies had become Champions. It is reported that, by this time, about five hundred Silkies had been imported. One of the first Champions was Milan Chips of Iradell and Milan Jenny Wren of Iradell, both having been imported from Australia. The first American-bred Champions were Iradell Peak A Boo and Coolaroo Janmar Marko. US Silkies are shown in a variety of activities such as Conformation and Obedience, Agility,

Am. Can. Int. Ch. Tawny Mist Copyright: The 1995 Pedigree and Iradell award winner, and a multiple Group winner in the US and Canada.

Photo courtesy: Donna Renton.

Herding and terrier go-to-ground trials. They are registered through the AKC and are awarded Championship, Obedience Trial Champion, Field Trial Champion and Agility titles through the AKC. They are considered to be a member of the Toy Group.

THE FIRST UK AUSTRALIAN SILKIES

It is known that Silkies arrived on British shores many years ago. Unfortunately they were not acknowledged as members of that breed. The public probably accepted them as Yorkshire Terriers, or even as mongrels, as the Silky was unknown in this country. Since then references to the Silky have been made in various books, including Hutchinson's *Dog Encyclopaedia*. This was at the time when these dogs were being called the Sydney Silky. As yet there are not many specialist books. Those that can be found are imported from America, Canada and Australia. In the book *Dogs of Australia*, in a section headed *Judging the*

Australian Silky Terrier, the first sentence reads: "First remember it is a Toy breed. Secondly remember it is a Terrier and must possess courage, keenness and strength." These are two points which are often forgotten.

In the mid-1970s Barbara Garbett, now deceased, imported Yatara Dutchboy (Connalee Regal Supreme ex Dutch Champion Kaylaw Samara, both Australian Imports) from Holland, and from Australia came Glenpetite Lolita (Milan Tramp ex Glenpetite Ena). Barbara's affix was Apico. At about the same time, Linda Stewart, of the affix Duskhunter, who was living down in Cornwall, imported a male from Australia, Glenpetite Wataboy (Milan Hugo ex Aust. Ch. Galacksi Petite Susie) and a bitch from Ireland, Coolmine Dockan (Vasterbackens Debut ex Albertina). At this time Barbara and Linda were unaware of each other.

It was in late 1979 that Anne Marshall saw her first Silky puppy. It was love at first sight. He was Apico Archie of Marshdae,

A garden party attended by members of the Australian Silky Terrier Society.

Photo: Russell Fine Art.

born on August 31st 1979 (Yatara Dutchboy ex Duskhunter Dolly at Apico). He introduced her, and many other people, to this endearing breed. Aussie, as he was affectionately known, was very nearly called Dumbo, after the elephant, because Anne's first impression of him was of a longish face, with huge ears standing straight up. Up until then Anne had been showing and breeding Yorkshire Terriers. Aussie looked so different.

In their determination to popularise Silkies, in 1979 Don and Barbara Garbett called a meeting of interested people. From this gathering a sufficient number of enthusiasts agreed to become founder members of a Breed Club. An inaugural meeting soon followed and in 1980 the Australian Silky Terrier Society was born. It held its first show in that same year. Further imports followed and in 1987 the Kennel Club gave official recognition by allocating the breed its own classes at Crufts.

Apico Archie of Marshdae (Yatara Dutchboy – Duskhunter Dolly), aged six months.

Photo: Marshall.

2 CHOOSING A SILKY TERRIER

The Silky Terrier is an active, outgoing and sound small dog, forever alert as to what is happening around and about. With these qualities the Silky has proved to be an excellent watchdog. A Silky is not a lap dog, and will bark, because the Terrier characteristic comes to the fore. The dog is compact, moderately low set, of medium length, with a refined structure. Silkies were bred originally to hunt and kill domestic rodents, and though they are still capable of performing this duty, unfortunately this ability is not as predominant as it once was. This has been brought about by the fact that the Silky is becoming more of a Toy dog than a Terrier, which many feel is to the detriment of the breed. People should be discouraged from purchasing a 'Miniature' Australian Silky Terrier, as this is definitely not a characteristic of the breed, nor is it a recognised breed. All Australian Silky puppies are born black and tan. As the dog matures the tan remains and, from approximately three to twelve months of age, their true colour materialises – that is blue and tan, or grey blue and tan, with a silver blue or fawn topknot.

THE CHARACTER OF THE SILKY

It would be a difficult task to find a breed that is more suitable as a companion in a home environment. Your puppy should have a temperament which enables him or her to fit into any situation, that is as a treasured family pet, or as a show dog. As a breed, Australian Silkies are very affectionate and have an enjoyment for living. When you have been away for any length of time, they are always eager to greet you, and are so happy to have you back home. Their 'glad to see you' attitude will brighten your day, and a few words of encouragement from you will see them running off in excitement. Also, in their own special way, they each have different ways of showing their affection. Some are 'waggers' – not just their tail but their whole body, especially when company arrives or you praise them for something they have done. Then there are the 'nuzzlers' – when they are in your company they will nudge you with their nose, just for you to pay attention to them. And then there are the 'mates' – no matter where you go, or what you do, they are always there beside you, investigating what you have done.

Silkies are a late-maturing breed, so it will

RIGHT: The Silky is a lively, affectionate dog, who will fit in with a variety of different lifestyles.

FACING PAGE: Gayplad Rumours are Fly'n (Aust. N.Z. Ch. Kamaroon of Kelbrae – Aust. Ch. Tarawera Dide Do Tu), pictured at eight months of age. Bred and owned by D.P. & T. Scales.

Photo: Cabal.

be two to three years before you have a fully-coated adult dog, with the true silky coat from which the name Silky derives. This coat is of a soft nature, and is nearly non-shedding, and for this reason the dog is always in great demand as a house pet because of the lack of the 'doggy odours' that are usually associated with hard-coated breeds. Silkies are great companions for people who suffer from allergies associated with dog hair. Although they are small dogs, Silkies are very agile, with the courage and tenacity of a Terrier or of a much larger dog. The Silky is an ideal watchdog, and is never afraid to tackle intruders, or much larger opposition. There are many stories of Silkies letting in visitors but holding the person up on the way out. For this reason alone they are in demand as a house pet. A well-known Toy judge and

breeder, Diane Banks, once summarised the Silky Terrier as being 'one of the most adaptable, hardy and fun-loving of breeds, who thrives on human company and are ideally suited for any home. What more could you want in one small bundle?'. A real package deal!

MALE OR FEMALE?

Before purchasing your new puppy you should make a decision as to whether you want a male or a female. Preference as to the sex of your puppy is a personal choice. Both sexes are much the same in disposition and character, and both make equally good pets.

GENERAL CARE

As a pet, the Silky is quite easily kept in a reasonable condition and just needs to be brushed, a few times weekly, with a widely-spaced bristle brush, and an occasional run-through with a steel comb. This grooming need not be a lengthy procedure, only a minute or so need be spent to keep your Silky in a satisfactory condition. For the show dog, however, more constant attention is necessary. Teach your children, even your toddlers, to handle your young Silky with all possible care. While they are very tolerant of children, kindness cannot be taught too early. Your new puppy is a healthy specimen, who will need a considerable amount of care and attention to remain in this condition and become a sociably acceptable specimen of the breed. More on the subject of care is covered in the chapter on Caring for your Silky Terrier.

FINDING A BREEDER

Successful breeders are people who spend time and money in establishing a high level of quality in their breeding, and who are prepared to use the best-quality stud dog, and the best-quality brood bitch, in an effort to produce a line of Silkies that are not only of excellent quality themselves, but will produce a better Silkies in the future. Such a person is indeed practising the 'art' of breeding, and can only then be said to be a true breeder. To find such a breeder, the best avenue would be to obtain a list of names and addresses from your national Kennel Club. When dealing with breeders, you should be aware of what you are paying for. Pure-bred puppies should come with a pedigree, and the relevant registration documents according to the stipulations of the national Kennel Club.

ASSESSING THE LITTER

Once you have contacted a breeder, and you have visited them to have a look at the puppies, it is essential that you make it clear why you want a puppy. That is, do you want your Silky as a pet, or are you looking for show quality? You must make the breeder aware of your requirements. When a litter is a pure-bred – that is, both parents are registered with their Kennel Club – pet puppies are sometimes the least expensive. Pet puppies are well-bred healthy puppies, but it is the opinion of the breeder that they are not suitable for breeding, or for the show ring, in comparison to the standard of perfection required for the breed. In general, only skilled breeders and judges can point out structural differences between a pet puppy and a potential show dog – and even then, they can get it wrong. It is important to emphasise the word 'potential' – no-one can guarantee that a promising puppy will fulfil that potential.

Having given this some thought, if you decide to show your puppy, make this clear to the breeder, who will help you select the best possible specimen of the breed. A show puppy may be more expensive than the pet puppy, but should be capable of competing in the show ring. One good tip when selecting a Silky Terrier is to take note of the inquisitive, outgoing pup, and make this part of the criteria for your selection. The puppy who comes up to greet you, and who seems curious and active is most likely an alert, healthy puppy.

PREPARING YOUR HOME

It is essential that you give a lot of thought to preparing your home for the new puppy, whether this is a pet, or a potential show puppy. Remember that the young puppy has just left mother, and will be a little upset. In their early days puppies will be affected by their surroundings, and this will have either a positive or a negative effect on their temperament in later years.

Silkies, being house dogs, do not need a lot of equipment, so try to obtain the necessities before bringing your puppy home. Providing a comfortable bed will solve half your problem of keeping the puppy off your lounges and your beds. Purchase a bed which is easy to clean, avoid hard-to-clean woven bases. Young puppies have a habit of chewing on their beds while they are teething, so avoid those made with plastic. Place some newspaper on the bottom – puppies from birth are raised on newspaper, and it may help them during the night to relieve themselves. For bedding use an old towel or blanket for warmth at one end of the bed. If you do not have a hot water bottle in the house, it would be an excellent idea to purchase one, as the young puppy will need to be kept as warm as possible.

Make the bed as interesting as possible with doggie toys, such as hard rubber bones or rings, and a rubber ball etc. Rawhide chew sticks will also occupy puppies, as well as acting as a teething ring while they are losing their baby teeth. Do not give them an old item of yours, like an old shoe, because they will not know the difference from an old and new one, so, when they chew on your new item and you chastise them for this, they will be confused. Place the bed away from the busy and noisy part of the house, to where it is cool in summer and warm in winter, and the puppy can settle down without being disturbed. Be sure that wherever you put your dog's bed, there are no electrical cords that can be chewed, or lamps that can be pulled over. While you are away from

home, having them in an area which will keep them out of mischief and out of harm is the ideal situation. After a while you will find that puppies very quickly learn that it is their sanctuary, and will go to it of their own accord for a rest.

Now that we have the bed and a few toys, you will need two feeding bowls, preferably metal (as the chew factor raises its head again, and puppies tend to destroy plastic ones), one for water and the other for food. While on the subject of food, consult with the breeder before you pick your puppy up, to give you a list of food that the puppy has been accustomed to, as a change in the diet could upset your puppy's stomach. Purchase what is required prior to bringing the puppy home, so that you will have it ready. If you so wish, you will be able to change your puppy's diet gradually, spread over a couple of days or weeks.

A stiff, wide bristle-brush, steel comb, tail comb, dog toenail clippers, nail file and a pair of round-ended scissors are all that is required to groom your puppy as a youngster and also as an adult. When purchasing a collar and lead, obtain one that you feel will suit the neck size of your puppy: don't make it too tight – that will distress the dog – or too loose so that your Silky can slip through it. These items should be purchased prior to bringing your puppy home, so that they are part of the environment from day one, which will make the settling-in period a lot easier.

COLLECTING THE PUPPY

When you take your puppy home from the breeder ask that you and other members of your family, are shown the correct way to pick up and hold the pup. A young puppy is very delicate and can be easily hurt. It is advisable to pick puppies up with one hand under their chest, and the other hand cupped under their back legs. It is a 'no no' to pull puppies up by the front legs, as this will damage their front legs by forcing them out at elbow. Damage could also be done to their shoulder joints. Once this damage is done, it is generally forever, so the need for the utmost care cannot be over emphasised.

If you have young children in the family it is a good idea to teach them the correct way to hold the puppy, by getting the children to sit down on the floor and placing the puppy in their laps. If the puppy should wriggle out of their hands, the subsequent fall will not be from a height that will hurt the puppy. All young pups are very active and will wriggle, so it is better to be safe right from the beginning. This is also a means of socialisation for the puppy and the child, and, if done correctly, they will form a bond that lasts for the life of the dog.

When collecting your puppy, have a box or travel crate ready in the car. It is advisable to always keep dogs protected in vehicles – they can be thrown around and badly injured if you have an accident, or have to brake quickly. Train them from a very young age on how you require them to behave in a car, if you intend taking them with you while travelling. One can imagine the disturbance to the driver if a puppy is allowed to travel loose in a car. Before leaving with your puppy, make sure that you have collected the necessary papers, i.e. the certificate of registration, the pedigree and the vaccination card signed by the vet.

SETTLING IN

Silkies, being very intelligent and affectionate, present you with much scope for development. Cultivate a friendship so that your puppy will want to please you. Teach your puppy his or her name early on. An appropriate name is more important than you think, so give plenty of thought to this. Make it simple, preferably one of a single syllable which can be easier to learn.

If you have young children in the family, they should be taught to treat the puppy with affection and care. It is likely that the puppy may not be accustomed to children. Teach your children to sit down on the floor and call the puppy by name. Most puppies will go to the children, but should this not happen, place the puppy up in the child's lap. Do not let children run at the puppies, bearing in mind that this would look, to them, like a giant coming towards them, and they will instinctively run the other way. Loud noises or banging, deliberately aimed at puppies, can make them unnecessarily nervous, and should be avoided.

It is only natural that children become over-excited when a new puppy arrives home, so be careful that it is not handled too much, as the puppy may become irritable and tired. Young puppies require a great deal of rest and sleep. Also teach your children not to go near, or touch, the feeding bowl while the puppy is eating, because most Australian Silkies will react to this being touched. By teaching your children to be gentle and kind, you will be helping to teach your puppy to be a sociably acceptable specimen.

Contrary to what a lot of people apparently seem to believe, Australian Silkies do get along very well with children, that is providing that the dog, from a very young age, is introduced into the family with children. As your Australian Silky matures, you will find that, being an active

Silkies get on well with children, providing introductions are made at an early age.

breed, the dog will love a play with the children, such as a game of ball, or a run. Do not expect the ball to come back – most times they will scurry away with the ball and hide it until later.

It will take a day or two for your puppy to get used to the new surroundings. Remember your Silky has just been separated from both mother and litter mates. A lot of kindness, understanding and patience is required here. The first night is usually the most disturbing for the whole family. The puppy may cry and howl, and seem to get very little rest. Put your pup into these new bedding arrangements early in the day, if possible, so that he or she will be able to adapt while it is light. Fondle your puppy, calm this nervousness, play together with the puppy's toys, and keep

your Silky well fed, comfortable and warm. Even then you may have to keep your puppy close by the side of your bed, or by the bed of older children.

Should your puppy still seem restless, it is advisable to place a hot water bottle wrapped in a towel, or with a covering over it, in the pup's bed, which will make up for the lost warmth of the litter mates. Do not use a heating pad or any other electrical appliance, as puppies do have a tendency to chew, which could result in electrocution. Also a loud-ticking alarm clock, or even a radio, placed in the room near the bed will be a comforting noise, and the puppy will not feel so alone. The puppy can usually be returned to the proper sleeping area by the second or third night.

3 CARING FOR YOUR SILKY

House training your Silky should not cause you too many problems. Silkies are remarkably clean dogs who will not want to dirty their own bed, so they will soon learn to let you know when they need to go outside. That is not to say that they do not have to be taught – although they are a highly intelligent breed, they do require instruction about where they should go.

The first step is to keep the puppy confined to an area of the house where you can watch, thus making training a lot easier for you. Preferably this area should be where the puppy's bed is placed. Most puppies are partially trained to newspaper before you buy them, as newspaper is used in their whelping boxes and is placed on the floor outside these boxes. This should make this part of training a bit easier for you. First, cover the entire floor with newspaper, except in the area in which you have located the bed, then watch the puppy carefully. You may notice the puppy sniffing the floor, crying, or running around in small circles. If this should be the case, pick your pup up quickly and place the puppy on the part of the newspaper you want to be used. Keep the puppy there until the

bladder and, if required, the bowels have emptied. Then do not forget the most important factor of this exercise – *praise*.

As the training progresses, gradually remove the newspaper until you have one small area in the corner. As this training process is going on during the first week or two, remove heavily soiled newspaper, but always leave one small damp piece, where the puppy can pick up the scent, which helps to lead the pup back to the newspaper next time. When you think the puppy is fairly consistent and has absorbed the idea of using the newspaper, you may feel at ease to let the puppy roam the house a bit, but keep an eye open.

Keep in mind the fact that, until your puppy is approximately five months old, neither the muscles nor the digestive system are under control, so you cannot expect too much. Normal, healthy, very young puppies will want to relieve themselves when they wake up in the morning, and after each feed, and after strenuous exercise. With puppies of six months and over, they will want to relieve themselves about an hour after each meal and just before bedtime. If there comes a time when you wish to train your puppy from newspaper to yard

Aust. Ch. Tarawera Dide Do Tu (Aust. Ch. Idem Ragtime – Tarawera Rubekah): Pictured at ten months, with Dayna Scales. If you take good care of your Silky, you will be rewarded with years of loving companionship.

Photo: Cabal.

training, it is a good idea to put a piece of damp soiled newspaper down in the yard. Once again the puppy's sense of smell will pick up the scent. Most puppies will perform in the yard with no hesitation.

While training puppies, you must remember, at all times, that you have to catch them in the act of breaking the training, otherwise the puppies will not know that they are being scolded for a break in their training. For instance, if you are angry and scold them as they are running towards you, they will immediately think that you are upset because they have come to you – next time you will have to

catch them. The idea of rubbing puppies' noses into their 'mistake' and then scolding them is wrong and of no value whatsoever. It is also unpleasant for both you and the puppy. If any puppy, at any time, makes it to the paper but only gets their front feet on it, never scold them for this because they think they are doing the right thing, and they should be praised, even though they have not done it perfectly.

It is not necessary to scold the puppy physically for breaking training; all that is required, when scolding a puppy, is a harsh tone of voice, and then take the puppy immediately to the newspaper or yard. As

Be firm, fair and consistent when introducing a young puppy to 'house rules'.

has already been stated, Australian Silkies are a highly intelligent and responsive breed, and their strongest desire is to please you, so your disapproval by scolding them in the correct manner is all that is necessary. Remember all the time that when they do something which is correct and pleases you, *praise* them lavishly, and they will perform as they should. Also, always remember to remedy puppies' mistakes on your floors by wiping them up immediately. A mixture of vinegar and water can be applied to hardwood floors or tiles, and the foam-type cleaners are helpful to use on carpets. Immediate action is needed in the case of urination, so that there is not a scent left for the puppy to pick up again.

Have a command to use when toilet training, such as "be quick". Start using this as soon as possible after the puppies have left the whelping bed. It is also worth reinforcing this command when outside and with adult Silkies – better to be safe than sorry!

Do not prevent puppies from hearing domestic household sounds such as the washing machine, the vacuum cleaner or a telephone ringing. The secret is not to make a fuss about the noise. If you ignore it, so will the puppies. It is only when a puppy is picked up in a hurried manner, when something occurs that the owner 'thinks' the puppy would be worried about, that the pup becomes apprehensive. Instead give lots of praise. While the puppies are listening to your voice, they will not hear the other noises going on around them.

FEEDING FROM PUPPY TO ADULT

As stated in Chapter Two, you will have already obtained a diet sheet outlining the food which the puppy has been accustomed to. If the diet must be changed, make sure that the change is gradual. Sometimes puppies develop diarrhoea when they move to a new home. This can be for several reasons – eating too much, eating foods that they have not been used to, or just an upset tummy caused by a change in routine. As long as the diarrhoea is not 'bloody' or goes on for too long – no longer than four hours – all should be well. Reduce the food a little, and make sure that the puppy has plenty of water, as

Gayplad Touch A Rainbow (Aust. N.Z. Ch. Kamaroon of Kelbrae – Aust. Ch. Tarawera Dide Do Tu), pictured at six months of age. Bred and owned by D.P. &T. Scales. By the time your Silky is six months old you should be feeding two meals a day, reducing to once a day by the time it is twelve months old.

Photo: Cabal.

dehydration can be a problem. If you are not able to obtain a diet sheet from the breeder, the feeding schedule from puppy to adult, detailed in this chapter, should be satisfactory.

When feeding young puppies, 'little and often' is the basic rule; do not distend their stomachs with food. Up to three months of age, your puppy should be having four meals a day. If, after three months of age, your puppy is still cleaning the plate quickly, it would be advisable to continue with the four meals a little longer. If your puppy begins to 'pick at' one of the meals, it usually is a sign that one meal can be stopped, thereby increasing slightly the size of the other three meals. From six months to one year, two meals. After a year, a dog does well on one meal a day. Puppies will rarely go a day without eating unless they are sick, but if your adult dog does not eat for a day, do not worry, unless they show signs of illness. If this is the case, consult your vet. Cow's milk should not be given to puppies, even if it is diluted, as it is very rich and high in fat. A good suggestion is equal parts Carnation milk and water, or some other form of tinned condensed milk, or double strength powdered milk, as young puppies have small stomachs and require concentrated food.

The well-known brands of canned and dry dog food on the market today are an excellent source of vitamins and minerals to promote a nutritionally balanced diet for your puppy and adult dog. There is a very large market for these products, and companies spend a great deal of money and research to produce a well-balanced product for your dog. If you wish to feed dry foods only, such as kibble and so on, you should add fat to the diet; these products are low in fat content so they will stay fresher longer.

There are a number of good food supplements on the market which supply the necessary vitamins and minerals for your dog. Vitamin D is well-known for its importance in the development of bones. Although not widely known, Vitamin D is also necessary for the proper utilisation of food in the gut. Low levels of Vitamin D are found in fresh lean meats. However, when canned foods are fed as the base to the diet, most of these contain added vitamins, including vitamin D. A deficiency of Vitamin D can cause rickets in growing pups. This causes weakening of the bones, which bend and distort as the pup grows. Aged dogs, particularly bitches, can suffer from another bone disease called osteomalacia. This results in loss of calcium from the bone and weakening of the bone

structure. Most of the canned and dry foods are fortified with calcium and Vitamin D to recommended levels. Check the ingredients on the can or bag to see if calcium and Vitamin D are listed. Vitamin K is a fat-soluble vitamin that can be stored in the body. Many of the complete dry foods contain Vitamin K at the daily required amount.

Fresh water should be available at all times for both puppies and adult dogs. Australian Silkies, both puppies and adults, take great delight in playing in their water, so one should always check their water-bowl three or four times a day. Clean water-bowls daily; a dirty water-bowl can be as much a source of contamination as the food bowl. Leave food for approximately 20 minutes, and then remove what the puppy has not eaten. Do not leave food lying around, as this can attract flies.

SUGGESTED PUPPY DIET
(up to three months of age)
Breakfast: Weetabix and milk
Lunch: Canned Puppy Food and grated cheese
Dinner: Canned Puppy Food and fresh lean mince
Supper: Milk (fat free).

SUGGESTED PUPPY DIET
(three months and over)
Morning meal: Weetabix with milk (fat free)
Afternoon meal: Combination canned and dry food
Evening meal: Same as afternoon meal.

GROOMING ROUTINE FOR THE PUPPY
Grooming is an essential part of your puppy's hygiene, and the amount is

A grooming routine should be introduced from an early age, and then your Silky will be quite happy to accept the attention.

Photo: Russell Fine Art.

A young Silky will need little exercise beyond the confines of the garden. As the dog gets older, he will enjoy as much, or as little, exercise as you can give.

minimal; no expensive clipping at the dog grooming salons, just frequent brushing at least twice a week by a member of the family is all that is required to keep your Australian Silky in top condition. The first step towards a healthy coat is general good health. Conditioning of the coat is essential, and the best method is a balanced diet of meat, vitamins and minerals, as described above. The puppy must be kept free of external and internal parasites (see the section on worming). If you forget to brush twice a week, and neglect the puppy for several weeks, it will take you twice as long to do the grooming when the time comes for it. Usually breeders have started puppy grooming, and for your puppy to continue to enjoy the grooming lessons, it is essential that they are performed on a regular basis. (See Chapter Four: Grooming and Coat Care.)

EXERCISE

There is not a great deal one can say on this subject for a young Silky puppy. During the first four months a puppy will get as much exercise as is needed within your own secure garden. It is advisable not to take a puppy out of these familiar surroundings, or to come in contact with strange dogs, until the puppy has had the final vaccinations. Taking a young puppy for a walk is not necessary until about six months of age. Lead training can take place in your own backyard in short spells, from three months of age. A collar left on for short periods can also help to accustom the puppy to the lead. Your Silky, once mature, will take us much exercise as you can give. Just remember, in very hot climates do not exercise or walk the dog on a hot road or path during the heat of the day. It would be just the same as if you walked without

shoes on – it would burn your feet, and that will happen with your dog.

VACCINATIONS

Although puppies acquire some protective antibodies from their mother through the first milk, the colostrum, this declines quite quickly, so that by the age of twelve weeks most puppies have lost their protection, particularly from distemper. The amount of protection puppies acquire, and hence the speed with which they lose it, depends on whether the mother has been given regular or recent vaccinations. Where the bitch has not been recently vaccinated, some vets and breeders advocate giving puppies a distemper vaccination at six to eight weeks of age as an added precaution. This is even more important if the puppies have not received any colostrum due to difficulties at birth. In most countries the normal age for receiving the primary vaccination is twelve weeks. From then on boosters will be required and your vet will advise you about when these should be administered. However, in Australia the first vaccination is usually given before you take your puppy home, which will be at approximately eight weeks of age. If that is the case, the breeder will give you the certificate of vaccination signed by a vet. If they do not give you one, this means that the puppy has not been vaccinated. In some cases a second vaccination is necessary at 12 weeks.

Make sure that your young puppy is healthy before you both leave the breeder – and by healthy one means that there are no discharges from the eyes. It is advisable to take your puppy to the vet for a check up as soon as possible after the puppy has arrived home, and arrangements can be made then for the vaccinations to be done. The young puppy's first vaccination is a temporary vaccination, which literally means that – temporary. The puppy can, and does, develop a certain level of immunity to the diseases against which the vaccines are given (Distemper, Hepatitis and Parvovirus), but there often is not enough immunity to withstand a strong challenge. For this reason you must not take your young puppy out of your own backyard until the second vaccination has been given, and the puppy must be kept away from areas frequented by other dogs.

The second vaccination will usually give them a fairly good immunity cover. The vaccine takes seven to ten days to reach its optimum level. After that you can start to take your young puppy with you on a few outings for socialisation. The third vaccination is most important. This is given at the time when the body is capable of producing a long-lasting response to vaccines. After the third vaccination has had time to take effect, you will be able to take your puppy with you and mix with other dogs. Remember the puppy has still be socialised, so make exposure to the outside world gradual. Puppies need to be vaccinated annually, as it is important to keep their level of immunity high. Vaccinations are also necessary if you wish to board your dog at any time while you are on holidays.

WORMING

In any worming programme there are two important facts to remember.
1. Worm eggs hatch in warm, humid weather. Worming should be regular, every six to eight weeks during this period. During the colder and drier weather, worming can be less regular, every three to four months.
2. Immature round and hook worms migrate through the body, and during this time, their first 10-12 days of their life cycle, they are not susceptible to worming preparations. Therefore, for the worming programme to be successful, it is advisable to worm your puppy twice for round and hook worm at a 10-14 day interval.

Start worming puppies at 10-14 days of age. Repeat once a week until six to eight weeks of age. Up to this age use either a worming cream, or syrup; from then on tablets can be used. After this, worm every two weeks until 14-16 weeks of age. From four months of age, worm every six to eight weeks, until one year of age. Puppies can have life-threatening quantities of round and hook worm as early as three weeks of age. They can also die by three to four weeks of age if they have heavy worm infestations.

Worm adults regularly at six-monthly intervals, although in some countries you might be advised to do it every three to four months. Use a broad-spectrum wormer, making sure that it is effective for all the species of worms liable to be found in your environment. It is sensible to take your vet's advice about worming programmes.

HEARTWORM

This is a problem in tropical regions where mosquitoes assist in the spread of this parasite; it is never by dog-to-dog contact. Mosquitoes that carry the infective larvae prefer warm, humid conditions, so the incidence of heartworm is far higher around river and coastal areas. Heartworm is now far more widespread than one would care to believe. With puppies, start treatment early in the mosquito season, at approximately three to four weeks of age, using a powder, liquid or tablets. If they are whelped during the winter months, start treatment at six to eight weeks of age. Dogs should be kept on a preventative all year round to be absolutely sure.

Adults and dogs over five to six months of age must first be tested by a vet before being given heartworm medication. A dog who is given heartworm tablets who already has heartworm, may show signs of toxicity – usually vomiting, occasionally jaundice, depression and lethargy. If this occurs, stop the tablets immediately and consult your vet. These signs may not show up for several months, or even longer. Once-a-month heartworm tablets are now available, and are proving popular for people who are erratic at giving the daily tablet, or if you go away frequently. If this is the case, then this form of preventative heartworm is for you. Try to establish a day in the month that is easily remembered, and use that date.

SOCIALISATION

As has been mentioned, your young puppy should not be taken out of your own backyard until after the second vaccination at 12 weeks of age. During the four weeks prior to this, it is a good time for the puppy to learn that everyday events, such as loud noises, squeaky toys and humans, are not harmful. This will be the beginning of the dog's life-long attachment to humans. Try to handle your puppy at least twice a day for say five to ten minutes. Sit together on the floor, allowing your puppy to crawl over you. Pick your puppy up to play with you.

In this early stage, this is vital to promote socialisation as, once the puppy is approximately seven weeks of age, the brain and nervous system have the capacity of an adult dog, but not the attention

The Silky is an intelligent little dog who will respond well to training.
Photo: Russell Fine Art.

capabilities. So the seven to twelve weeks of age stage is the best time for man-dog socialisation, where your young puppy, by receiving individual attention, will become self-sufficient as an individual, rather than one of the mob in a litter where the more dominant puppy usually takes over. Also concentrate on lead training during this period. Firstly leave a collar on for approximately one hour a day, so that the puppy accepts the fact of having something around the neck. Once the puppy stops scratching at the collar, and becomes accustomed to it, you can then attach a lead and spend time lead-training in your own backyard.

After 12 weeks of age we commence another stage of development and socialisation. Training should still be limited to 10 to 15 minutes at a time, as puppy's attention span is still limited. After 16 weeks it is time for expanding the puppy's ability to accept things that are not normal. By this one means socialisation with the general public, by taking the puppy to shopping centres, open weekend markets and friends' places. The puppy will encounter different noises, traffic, shapes and sizes. Do it gradually, not all in one day. Socialising your puppy is never wasted: it makes for a more manageable dog that will become a delight to own.

EARLY TRAINING LESSONS

A few points to remember when training your puppy.

1. Teach one exercise at a time before going on to the next one.

2. All exercises are taught by repetition. Kindness (pats and play times) and rewards (little snacks) are given after each session.

3. When training your puppy, use a strong voice, give commands in a firm clear tone. Once you have given a command, persist until it is obeyed, even if you have to pull the dog to obey you. The puppy must learn the difference between training and playing – that when a command is given in a firm clear voice it must be obeyed.

4. Be consistent with the use of words during training, and restrict them to as few as possible, and never alter them. Use commands like 'Come', not 'Come over here', and 'Walk', not 'Let's go for a walk'.

5. It is best for one person to carry on with the puppy's training.

Training is hard on the puppy and the owner, and as the puppy's attention span is still limited, at first it should not be longer than five to ten minutes at a time. Gradually increase the length of time to about 30 minutes. As the session time lengthens, you will find that you will become impatient and possibly lose your temper. If this happens, stop the session immediately and resume at another time. After each training session it is very important to have a play period; *never* play during training.

THE CANINE GOOD CITIZEN TEST

These schemes are organised by the various national Kennel Clubs. Launched in the US, they are now widespread, and they are eminently suitable for all dogs and their owners. Basic training is given, culminating in a final test when the dog and owner pass out as 'Good Citizens'. The scheme started in America, and has been slightly adapted for use in Britain.

THE UNITED STATES

The exercises include:

1. Accepting a friendly stranger: To demonstrate that the dog will allow a friendly stranger to approach and speak to the handler in a natural everyday situation.

2. Sitting politely for petting: To demonstrate that the dog will allow a friendly stranger to touch him while he is out with his handler.

3. Appearance and grooming: To demonstrate that the dog will welcome being groomed and examined and will permit this to be done by a stranger.

4. Out for a walk with the dog on a loose leash: To demonstrate that the handler is in charge of the dog.

5. Walking through a crowd: To demonstrate that the dog can move about politely in pedestrian places and is under control in public places.

6. Sit and Down on command/Staying in place: To demonstrate that the dog will respond to the handler's commands to "Sit" and "Down", and will remain in the place commanded by the handler.

7. Praise/Interaction: To demonstrate that the dog can be easily calmed following play or praise.

8. Reaction to another dog: To demonstrate that the dog can behave politely around other dogs.

9. Reactions to distractions: To demonstrate that the dog is confident at all times when faced with common distracting situations.

10. Supervised isolation: To demonstrate that a dog can be left alone, if necessary.

BRITAIN

The exercises include:

1. Putting a collar and lead on your dog.

2. The dog must walk on a lead without distraction; the dog should walk steadily on the left side of the handler.

3. The dog and handler must walk through a door or gate.

4. The dog must be on a lead and ignore other dogs and people, waiting quietly while the handler holds a conversation for one minute.

5. The dog, with lead attached, must be left by the handler for one minute at a distance of five metres – the handler remains in sight. This exercise does require a fair degree of training.

6. The dog must stand steady while being groomed.

7. The handler presents the dog on a lead for examination, and the examination includes mouth, teeth, throat, eyes, ears and feet.

8. The handler releases the dog from the lead, the dog is allowed to play, and is then recalled and the lead is attached.

If the dog receives a 'Passed' category against every exercise a Canine Good Citizen test certificate is awarded. The tests are carried out by suitably qualified people. Some obedience and training clubs are now training dogs and owners to pass the Good Citizen Scheme, and breed clubs are being encouraged to take part. Taking part in this scheme should ensure a well-behaved pet, and also, of course, the satisfaction of winning a certificate.

It can be very useful to train your puppy to travel in a cage – some use these as sleeping quarters. They are essential for dogs travelling by car, train and air. Most show dogs are transported to and from shows by this method.

4 GROOMING AND COAT CARE

As the name suggests, Silkies have a fine, silky, strong coat which sheds very little. It is a good idea for you, the owner, to start training your puppies for grooming sessions early in their lives. You can start this from day one. When inspecting your litter, turn each puppy on to its back on the blanket, or in your hand. Hold the puppy there for a short time, talking and giving praise. Of course the puppies cannot hear you as yet, but they can feel vibrations through their tiny bodies. As they grow, hold them in your arms, still on their backs, in a "cradle" position. Try to do this each time you pick them up as part of a handling routine. While they are in this position you can run your fingers over their bodies, hold a foot, tickle a tummy, so that the puppies soon become accustomed to being touched. It must be for different lengths of time, so as not to programme them. When the time comes to trim nails, or trim the hair round the foot, the job is much easier to perform if the puppy is used to being in this position. Training must be carried out in a calm manner, without any fuss. Talk to the puppies quietly, tell them what they are to do, using short, simple terms, for example

"lie down" (on their backs), "stand", "no" etc. Change the tone of your voice. Dogs and puppies will come to a high-pitch singsong voice, rather than one coming from your boots. The latter tone has its place should you have to reprimand them. Introduce their names (if you have decided on them). They will soon gain confidence in what you want to do, and lie there quite content, listening to the sound of your voice.

Silkies enjoy being groomed – as has previously been stated, they love attention. If you happen to catch a knot and pull the hair, the puppy will cry; so stop and pet the puppy. Let the puppy know that it was an accident by making an affectionate fuss – and maybe a small piece of dog biscuit offered as a treat will ease the pain. If you are rough, and scold the puppy for pulling away, the puppy will start to dislike the grooming sessions very quickly. Likewise, if you are gentle and patient, the puppy will enjoy being brushed. As with all training, you must be firm, teach your puppy what is required, and give lots of praise when the puppy does what is correct. Silkies are a breed with a high degree of intelligence and, as a result, if you let them get away

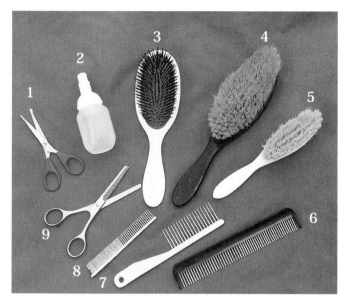

GROOMING STEP BY STEP
Photos by Russell Fine Art.

The grooming kit.

1. *Round-ended scissors;*
2. *Spray water-bottle;*
3. *Firm bristle brush;*
4. *Soft bristle brush;*
5. *Baby/head brush;*
6. *Comb – rotating teeth;*
7. *All-purpose comb;*
8. *Fine-medium comb;*

with something once, they will soon rule you. So it must never be said that Silky will not let you groom them, because if that is the case it is because the owner has not persevered and trained the puppy to be groomed properly. Silkies also, being active dogs, are wrigglers, so you will have to hold them firmly.

Start grooming by gently stroking the baby brush over the body. The puppy will try to play with the brush at first. Don't scold – the puppy does not know this is wrong. Just tell the puppy 'no', letting the word continue on – 'no........o' – in a much deeper voice, then quickly call the puppy's name in a bright and breezy manner. The importance of the tone of your voice when training dogs cannot be emphasised too frequently; it is through this that they know whether they have done something right or wrong. They can also tell whether you are pleased or otherwise.

Puppies must learn to stand on a table, or whatever surface you intend to brush them

on. Use a firm table on which you have placed a mat to prevent the puppy slipping; and old bath mat is useful for this. It is important that puppies are happy on the table. If they feel their legs slipping from under them, they will not stand correctly. Of course, if you intend to show your young puppy, the exercise of standing on a table is of the utmost importance, as puppies are required to stand on a table to be examined by a judge for conformation. It is a good idea to use a coffee table, when training puppies to stand on a table, as it is not far to the ground if they try to jump off.

Using your brush and long firm strokes, brush the coat from the parting to its length, brushing right through to the skin. This stimulates it, thus promoting hair growth. It also produces a beautiful shine to the coat. When you are happy with this process, dampen the coat slightly. This aids grooming. Boiled rain-water is best, or tap water, or a prepared coat grooming aid. If

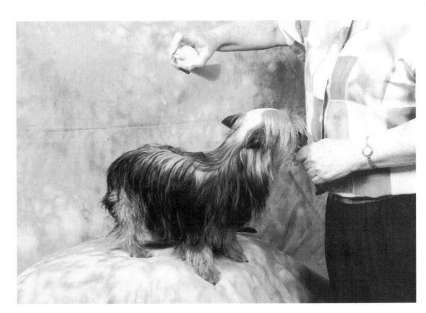

When grooming a dry dog, dampen the coat or spray with an anti-tangle preparation. Make sure you shield the dog's face when spraying.

you suspect there are any tangles then add either a little conditioner to the water, or use a small amount of an anti-tangle product. By doing this you will not be damaging the coat any more than necessary.

THE HEAD

Start with the head. Brush back the hair on each side of the muzzle, in the direction of growth. Some Silkies have short hair on their muzzle and feet. These are referred to as being 'clean pointed' and will require very little attention, while others will need to have some hair removed to produce the required effect and meet the requirements of the Breed Standard, which states that long hair on the foreface or cheeks is very objectionable, ears should be entirely free from long hair, and legs from knees and hocks to feet should be free from long hair. Your Silky must have a clean trim on muzzle, ears and feet. If your Silky is trimmed five days before a show then the

muzzle, ears and feet will have a clean, velvet look.

Excess hair can be removed from the muzzle, ears and feet by any of the following methods, and you can decide which suits you and your Silky best:–

1. By trimming with scissors. Thinning scissors can give a satisfactory finish, although some breeders do not agree with this method and maintain the only place on which to use scissors is when trimming between the toes and trimming the tail.

2. By using clippers. Some breeders consider this is the best way, using a good set of hand clippers and a small pair of cordless, battery-run, pet trimmers. Others feel these leave an exaggerated finish, one which does not look natural.

3. By plucking with your fingers. This method promotes new growth and encourages a stronger colour. Many people feel that this is the superior method and gives a nicer, more natural finish. On the other hand some people consider it is old-

THE HEAD

LEFT: Trimming the muzzle: Thinning scissors can be used to remove excessive hair between shows.

BELOW LEFT: The whiskers and the hair over the eyes are checked for length.

BELOW: If necessary, thinning scissors can be used to trim the hair to the correct length, giving a more finished look.

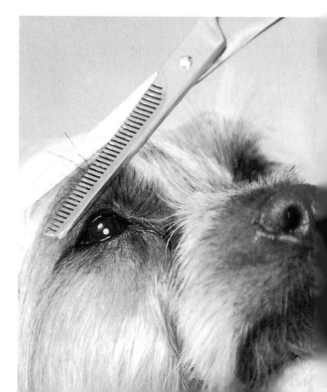

fashioned and prefer the clippers.

It is a good idea to explain how the plucking method is done. Using finger and thumb, hold a few hairs, no more than three or four, and gently pull them out. There is no need for any tugging or harsh movement. The hair being removed is dead and breaks off easily. You are not pulling the hair out of the skin, the hair breaks naturally. There can be a few dogs and groomers that this method would not suit. The alternative method would be to use the thinning scissors. Carefully work from the nose to the lip down each side; always have the scissors pointing downwards, away from the eyes. Be careful and cut just the ends off the coat. Do not cut right back to the corner of the mouth, but about half way. The finished result would leave the nose, over the bridge, up to the inner corner of the eye, to about half to three-quarters the way along the upper lip, free from long hair. Sometimes there is a need to cut off the whiskers, using scissors, to clean the muzzle. Brush the hair from above the eyes between the ears down the back of the neck. This will encourage the hair not to hang over the face, which is objectionable – the eyes must be visible at all times. Now brush under the chin and down the chest. Never trim hair from this part.

THE BODY COAT

Brush the hair from the centre back down each side, in one action to length. Never bring the brush away from the body towards the end of the coat, as this would encourage the hair to flick out. The hair must hang flat and straight at all times. Make sure you are brushing right through the coat. It may be necessary to have the dog lying on its back, or to hold up the front paws, while you brush the underbody.

DEALING WITH TANGLES

If you come across a tangle, deal with it at once. This is done by holding the hair as close to the skin as possible. Then, with your fingers, or the first two teeth of a wide-toothed comb, gently break up the tangle almost hair by hair. A small amount of conditioner on the tangle allows the hairs to slide apart more easily. Continue to brush through carefully, after making sure that it is all clear. If the knots have been there for any length of time and they need to be cut, use your round-ended scissors to cut lengthwise in the same direction as the hair grows; do not cut across the hair. And be aware – a lot of dogs will warn you about tangles by starting to fidget if they think you are about to find one. They seem to know exactly where they are. The most likely place for knots is around the base of the ears, under the front legs and inside the back legs.

THE PARTING

While the dog is in the standing position, following a thorough grooming, brush the hair from behind the dog's ears, down the body, following the line of the spine to the tail. If this is done in a straight line you will find that the coat parts itself. This can be encouraged by brushing the hair to each side of the parting. This method is a lot easier than trying to run the end of a tail comb down the centre, and it works well, especially on a damp coat. However, you might prefer to use the end of a tail comb to achieve the parting, though combing a straight line requires co-operation between you and your dog.

The centre parting is difficult to achieve on young puppies, as their hair is usually

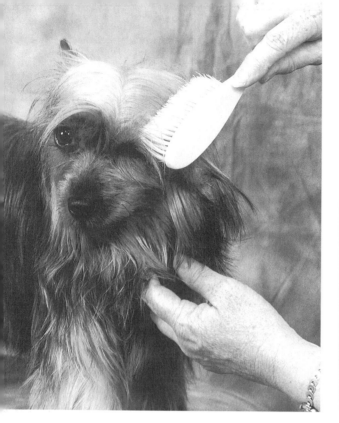

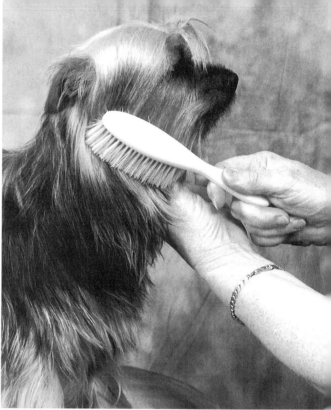

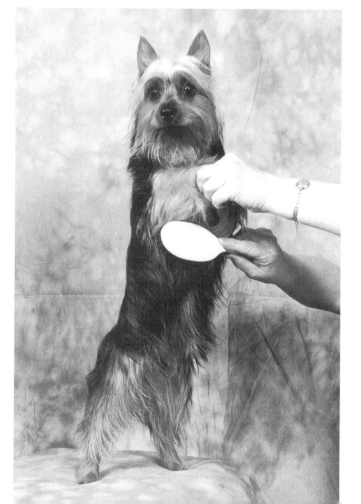

TOP LEFT: Brush the head coat to each side of the head to start the parting.

ABOVE: Continue to brush the coat down each side of the face.

LEFT: Brush under the body, holding the feet up.

THE PARTING

Brush down the back, following the spine to create the parting.

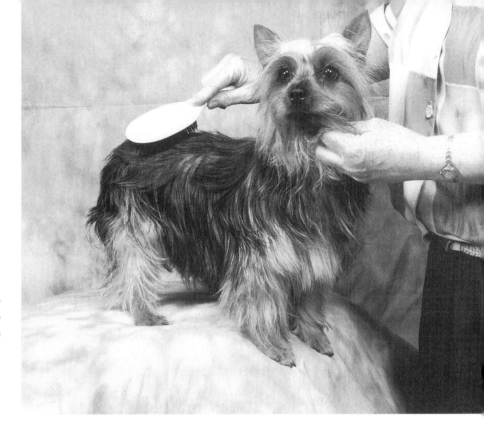

Brush the body coat down from the parting to create a straight coat.

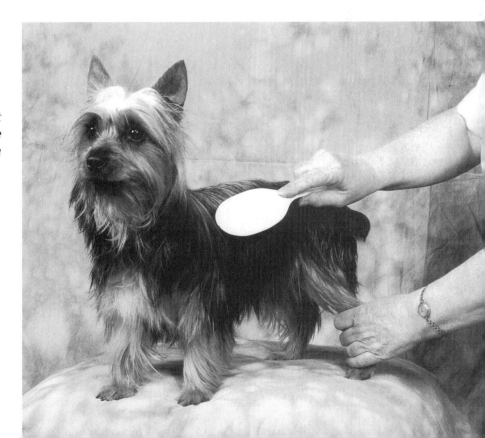

too short to lie flat. As the coat grows, the hair will have a natural tendency to make a centre parting, and the weight of the coat will help it lie flat. Do not brush the hair over the eyes, but separate the hair to the front and back of the ears, so the ears stand erect between the separation. Now that you have achieved the parting, especially on the head, your young puppy will shake itself but, after doing this three or four times, will usually give in. Mind you, some never do, and will always give themselves a good shake. When the hair is longer, its length will help it fall back into place after the puppy has indulged in some head-shaking. Occasionally check the length of the coat. Remember, we should see daylight under the coat, and the feet should always be visible. If there is a need to remove a little, do so with the thinning scissors – but, remember, no straight lines!

THE EARS

The size of the ear can be visually changed by the amount of hair taken off the ear flaps. If they are too big, then you would leave more hair on nearest to the head. Do not forget that the ears should be pointed, not rounded off. You will find some hair does grow inside the ear canal. This should be carefully plucked out, hair by hair, leaving the canal clean. Many dogs scratch their ears due to irritation caused by these hairs and, while they are scratching, they are breaking coat. Wipe out the ears with flexible cotton buds. This will also prevent the accumulation of wax, which can irritate the ear and promote scratching. Do not probe too deep into the ear. There are ear drops which will remove wax by bringing it to the surface, which then just requires wiping clean, thus removing any need to probe. Ask your vet about this. The trimming of the ear and ear care is very important in young puppies, in order to help the ears stand erect. They can have their ears up one day and down the next, which is caused by teething, but if they have a lot of hair on their ears, the weight of this will prevent the muscles in the ear gaining the necessary strength to stand erect. The finished result of your work should be a smooth, velvety appearance of short hair.

Excess hair is removed from the back of the ear-flap between shows.

The thinning scissors method is used to shorten the hair on the foot between shows.

THE FEET

Another area which should be void of long hair is the feet. The length of the hair round the feet should be equivalent to that on the muzzle. Using your preferred method, remove all long hair from below the hock/ankle to the ground. For a young puppy a minimum amount of trimming is necessary, but it is suggested that it be done on a regular basis. Hold your young puppy on your lap while you do this trimming. Using your round-ended scissors, trim the long hair between the pads of the feet. It is important to keep this hair out from between the pads of the feet, otherwise it will cause the feet to spread, and, if you intend showing your young puppy, this is even more important, as the standard calls for 'cat-like' feet with closely-knit toes. This hair can also harbour small stones which would cause sore feet and lameness. Proceed slowly, to avoid cutting one of the footpads. Then stand your dog on a firm

table and brush the hair on top of the foot in the opposite direction of growth, then trim round the foot, with round-ended scissors, leaving a clean appearance. Many dogs are sensitive round their pads; so have patience, reassure the dog that all is well. Sometimes rubbing the area with your finger, then with the closed scissors, alleviates all fears.

The nails need trimming if they touch the floor while the dog is standing squarely. Once again, hold the dog on its back in your lap and, using your toe-nail clippers, take a little bit of nail at a time. If trimming nails bothers you, get a groomer to do it. If you accidentally draw blood, you can put flour on the tip of the nail to stop the blood flow, or you can consult your vet about the medication available to stop bleeding. You may find it easier to file your young puppy's nails, and this can be done whenever you have your Silky in your lap.

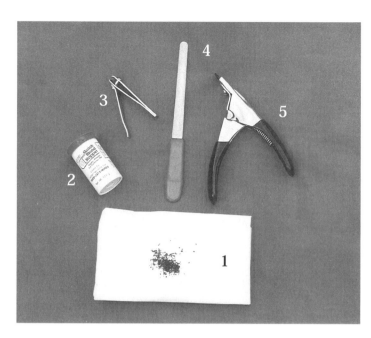

Nail trimming equipment

1. Potassium permanganate;

*2. Styptic powder
(1. and 2. are both used to
stop bleeding from the nail);*

*3. Small nail-clippers
(human type used on
puppies' nails);*

4. Nail file;

*5. Nail-clippers (guillotine
type).*

*Nails should be
trimmed, taking care
you do not cut into
the quick. The blade
must be sharp to
prevent leaving a
jagged edge.*

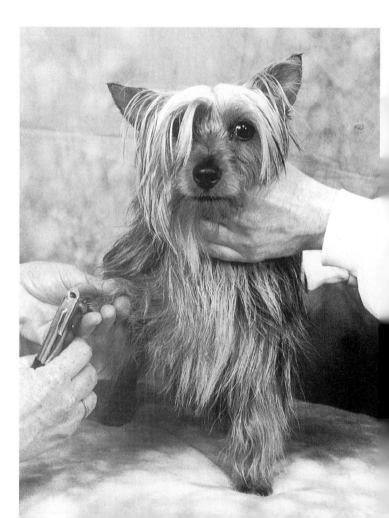

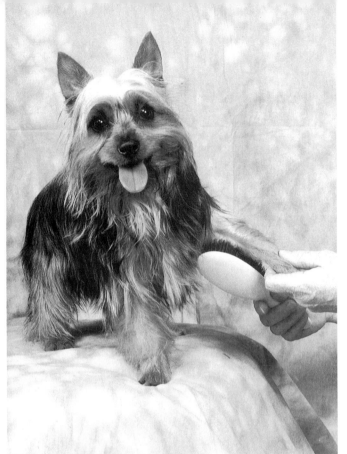
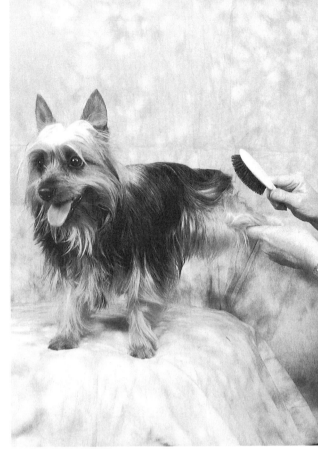

THE LEGS

ABOVE: Brush each leg in turn.

BELOW: Comb through the hair on the legs to ensure there are no tangles.

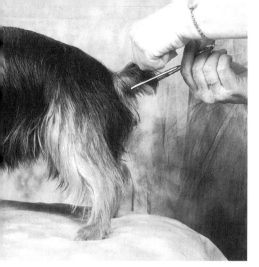

THE TAIL

ABOVE LEFT: The coat underneath the tail may need to be shortened periodically.

ABOVE RIGHT: Don't forget to brush the tail furnishings.

THE LEGS

The leg hair above the foot should be well groomed. Brush upwards then down, or side to side. Make sure the leg hair does not hide the feet when the dog is standing.

THE TAIL

This should also be free from long feathering but should be well-coated. Therefore you should trim off the long hair, that is any hair which is over a quarter of an inch long, using thinning scissors. The best way to is comb the tail hair down each side of the tail, then trim away, from under the tail, leaving the nice dark blue coated tail at your preferred length. There have been questions asked as to what we would do with a full length tail. Some views are that we should trim. Others would prefer to leave the long coat on the tail – but not for showing.

THE JAWS AND TEETH

The jaw should be strong, the teeth even and clean. Teeth should never be neglected. If a dog has a suitable balanced diet, this will contain the calcium and vitamin D required to produce strong, white teeth.

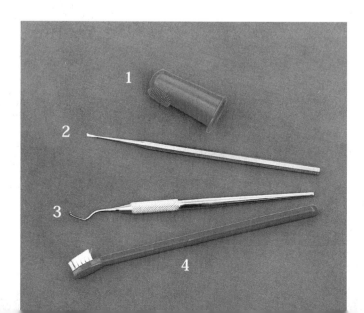

THE TEETH
*Teeth-cleaning
equipment.*

*1. Finger-brush;
2. Tooth scaler (type 1);
3. Tooth scaler (type 2);
4. Dog toothbrush.*

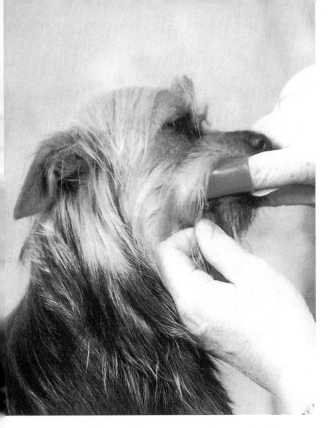

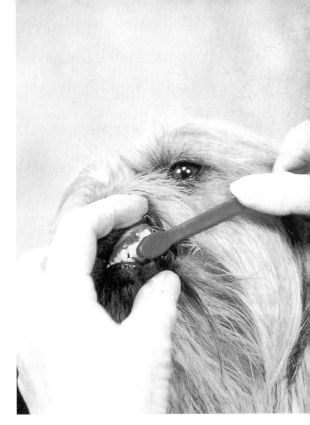

ABOVE: Cleaning the teeth with a finger-brush.

*BELOW: If tartar accumulates on the teeth they will
need to be scaled.*

*ABOVE: Cleaning the teeth with a specially designed
dog toothbrush and paste.*

*BELOW: A Silky with the correct scissor bite, and well
cared-for teeth.*

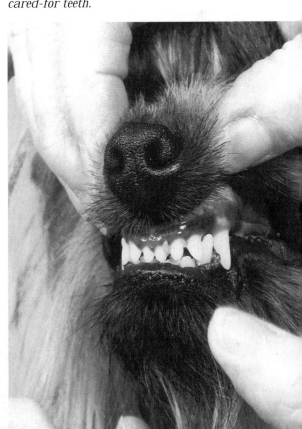

The use of a lemon will also help to clean teeth. If you allow tartar to build up, this pushes the gum away, causing infection of the gum and/or the teeth. Silkies' teeth are not generally a problem. They can start to shed their teeth at about seven years of age but some keep them for much longer. Teeth should be checked regularly in young puppies to see that the baby teeth come out as they should. The permanent teeth begin coming through at four to six months of age, and in some cases the baby teeth do not fall out, and you can have two sets of teeth. This problem occurs most often with the canine teeth (fangs) at the front corners of the mouth. If they are not loose enough to come out, you should have your vet extract them.

EYE CARE

Silkies do not usually suffer from eye staining or watery eyes, unless there is something irritating in the eye. It is so easy for something like grass seed, or a small piece of grit, to get into the eye. The natural defences come into operation, producing tears which should wash away the foreign body. But eye drops are available, should they be required. If in any doubt, let your vet examine the eyes. They are such fragile parts and require special treatment. There are a number of different products which claim to remove tear staining but you *must* read the small print before trying any of them out.

BATHING

Avoid bathing your young puppy until all the inoculations have been given, and be sure your Silky is not chilled when being bathed or in the process of drying. Two people rarely agree as to how often dogs should be bathed. Some do not like to bath them too often, claiming that it removes the natural oils. Yet others bath their dogs every two weeks, sometime even more often. It depends on the type of life your dog leads. Ones which lie and roll in just about everything will obviously require frequent washes. Grooming a dirty dog will do more harm to the coat than bathing it, and there are preparations which can be applied to the coat to prevent coat breakage, one of these being lanolin. A show dog should be bathed for each show. It would be impolite not to do so. The judge expects to be presented with a clean, well-groomed dog, not one you just put a lead on and take to a show. It would also be an insult to the dog if you had not made sure that he, or she, were at their usual gleaming best. Silkies look a million dollars walking round the ring as if they owned it, demanding that you look at them.

You will need bath-time equipment. As far as shampoos are concerned, there are so many different types that it becomes a matter of personal choice. There are some who prefer to share with their dogs the shampoo they themselves use – after all, a Silky's coat is much like our own hair. They avoid, however, using a shampoo and conditioner combined, preferring to be able to control how much of each is used, and so purchase separate shampoos and conditioner. It is advisable to use baby shampoo for puppies, and for the faces of older dogs, as this is much kinder on the eyes. Conditioners, like shampoos, come in a wide variety, with each one claiming to be for a different hair type. You may require different ones for each dog, to give the required result. Dogs are like us, so do not use the same type even in one family. The secret is to try them out, but not when washing for a show. Remember to *read the*

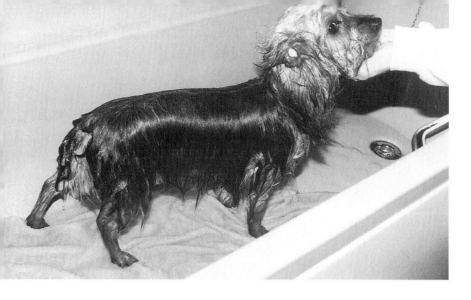

BATHING

Bathtime: The first soaking. Note the towel in the bath to prevent the dog from slipping, and the cotton-wool in the ear to prevent water or soap from getting in.

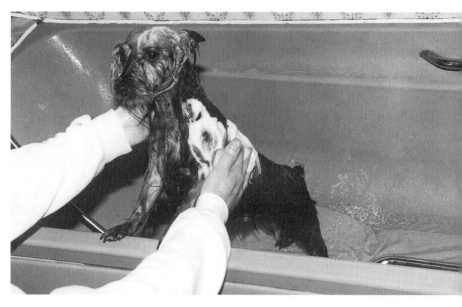

The shampoo is applied, working it into a rich lather, without disturbing the coat.

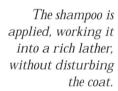

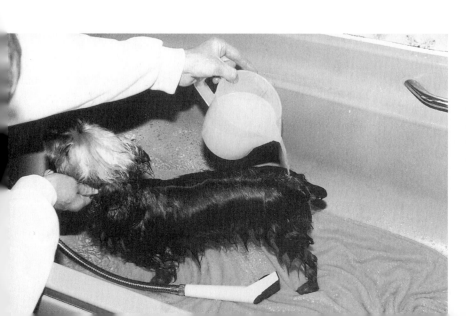

Rinse aid is applied, after the shampoo has been rinsed out.

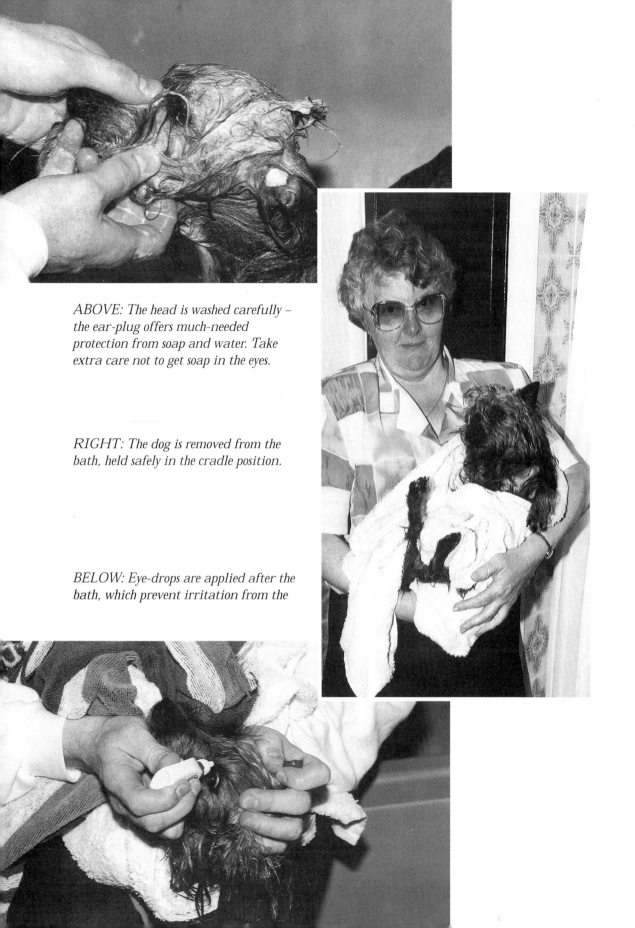

ABOVE: The head is washed carefully – the ear-plug offers much-needed protection from soap and water. Take extra care not to get soap in the eyes.

RIGHT: The dog is removed from the bath, held safely in the cradle position.

BELOW: Eye-drops are applied after the bath, which prevent irritation from the

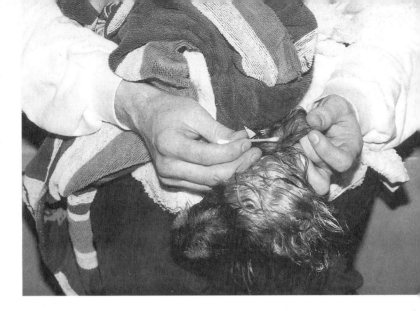

The ears are cleaned following the removal of the ear-plugs. Take care not to probe into the ear canal.

instructions on both the shampoo and conditioner bottles before using them.

You will need towels – large bath sheets are best because they can be folded in half for more absorption. You will need one per dog. You need a bath mat to prevent the dog slipping in the bath, or an old towel will do. Then you must have clean grooming equipment – what is the point of bathing a dog then grooming with dirty equipment? And have a small amount of cotton wool, or cotton, handy for placing in the ears to prevent water entering them. Eye drops may be used, before and after bathing, to protect the eyes. There are a number of homoeopathic and herbal products available, including one for eye treatment. They are much safer than many other products, unless ones have been prescribed for you by your vet. And, finally, clean paper and/or bedding are necessary. Before bathing, clean ears then apply cotton plugs, put eye drops in and clean teeth by using either a toothbrush, or a finger brush or by scaling using a tooth scaler. Presumably you will be using your bath in which either to bath or shower your dog, although there are specially made dog baths. Alternatively, if you have a very large

sink, that would be just fine. Without a shower you could use jugs of warm water. Use plastic ones, as these will be less noisy. Obviously you will need a good supply of warm water. Prepare the shower prior to putting the dog in the bath. It must be luke-warm water. Wet the dog's body first. Apply a small amount of shampoo and wipe this into the coat. Do not ruffle the coat as this could cause tangles. Try to keep the coat flat. Dilute the shampoo 50/50 with water – this makes it easier to work into the coat and quicker to rinse out. If you dilute your shampoo with warm water it is not such a shock when it is applied; otherwise it will feel very cold on the dog's warm body.

Rinse out thoroughly, then wash the head with baby shampoo. Try to train your dogs to keep their noses up, then the water does not run into them. Apply conditioner, comb through and rinse out. Do be sure that all the shampoo and conditioner is removed from the coat, otherwise you will not be pleased with the end result. Allow your dog to shake off the excess water before being removed from the bath. If the ear plugs do not come out during this shaking they must be removed. Then clean the ear canal with cotton buds, but take

51

After getting out
as much water as
you can, lie the
dog on his back
and groom the
underbelly.

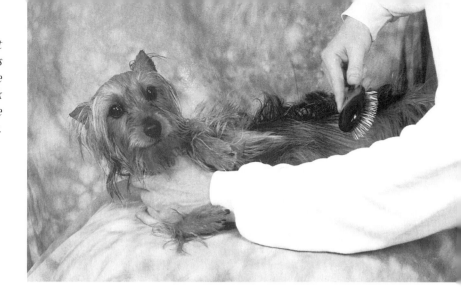

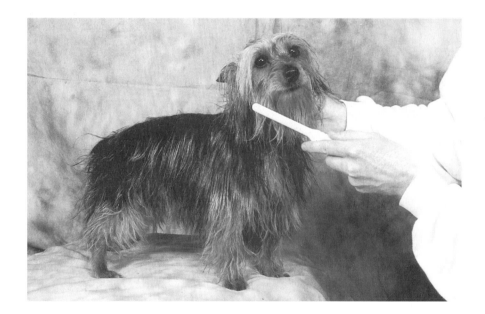

Groom the
head prior
to drying.

A hand-held
hairdryer can be
used, making sure
the hair is always
blown
downwards.

RIGHT: Use the comb with rotating teeth to tidy up.

BELOW: This young dog has had a lanolin coat-dressing applied following bathing. This will prevent coat tangles and hair loss – the dressing will be bathed out prior to the show.

*Marshdae Whata Chance to Dream:
The fully-groomed Silky.*

care. Wrap the dog in a warm towel and squeeze out as much water as you can. Stand the dog on a table. A lot of people like to have the dog standing throughout the drying process so as not to create unwanted creases in the coat. Brush, then comb, through the whole coat, doing a section at a time. You may find it easier to start at the ends, and then work gradually up to the roots.

It is perfectly acceptable to use a hand-held dryer. You do not require a very hot temperature, but you do need to be able to vary the speed. When drying, always hold the dryer so that the hair is blown downwards. If you allow the coat to fly about during drying, it will not lie flat when finished. Brush through while drying – this will produce a straight coat. Start at the head, as no dog likes having a wet face for very long and they will try to rub it in the towel. Then work down each side, again working in sections, round the body, until the hair is dry. You may need to hold the dog up to dry and groom underneath. Check that the whole body is dry, including the tail and legs, otherwise, when the dog curls up to sleep, the hair will crease, giving a wave effect. This is most undesirable.

If you have a number of Silkies to prepare for a show, you may like to have a stand which will hold the dryer for you, leaving both your hands free. If your dogs will not stand still while being groomed, there are frames to which you can fasten their leads; again this leaves your hands free to groom. The finished result should be a picture – a gleaming, beautiful Silky.

5 THE BREED STANDARDS

The Australian Silky Terrier should be a glamorous little dog, with refined outlines, but it must not be forgotten that Silkies were originally bred principally as hunters and killers of domestic rodents. This, of course, immediately dispels any image of weediness, yet should impart an impression of agility and speed. The 'Keen Alertness and Activity' qualities required will not allow for a nervous, temperamental little dog. He should, in all ways, be balanced; the head not being so broad and heavy as to necessitate a heavy body. His head should be basically wedge-shaped (tapering more than that of a Yorkshire Terrier, with less stop and less prominent cheek bones). He should not be snipy in the muzzle, a condition often found with cramped or missing teeth. His body coat length balances with the overall dog. On some specimens a 12.7 cm (5 ins.) coat is more than ample, while others need every bit of the 15.2 cm (6 ins.). The comments on colour are of a general nature, as it is a much wiser move to err in the area of which 'Blue' might be more correct, rather than in that which is the sounder, more stylish exhibit. Of course, with specimens equally typical, the richer colour must reign supreme. At a glance the Silky should appear to have a refined outline, to be a little long rather than cobby, but this must not be exaggerated, as the Standard states 'moderate' length, with refinement. The tail carriage can alter the whole appearance of the animal, and so an erect tail carriage, of any degree, is usually preferred to a dropped tail. The latter is usually indicative of a nervous temperament.

The preparation and grooming of the exhibit is of the utmost importance in this breed, as the Standard specifically requests 'a well-groomed appearance'. This is a statement not made in any other Toy Standard, and so particular attention should be paid to the manner in which each exhibit is presented.

THE AUSTRALIAN BREED STANDARD

GENERAL APPEARANCE The dog is compact, moderately low set, of medium length with a refined structure but of sufficient substance to suggest the ability to hunt and kill domestic rodents. The parted, straight silky hair

presents a well-groomed appearance.

CHARACTERISTICS It should display Terrier characteristics, embodying keen alertness, activity and soundness.

HEAD Of moderate length, slightly shorter from the tip of the nose to between the eyes than from the same position to the occiput. The head must be strong and of Terrier character, being moderately broad between the ears; the skull flat and without fullness between the eyes, with fine, silky topknot, not falling over the eyes (a long fall of hair on the foreface or cheeks is very objectionable). Nose black.

EYES Shall be small, round, not prominent, dark as possible in colour with a keen intelligent expression.

EARS Should be small, 'V'-shaped with fine leather, set high on the skull, pricked, and entirely free from long hair.

MOUTH Strong jaws, teeth even and not cramped, the upper incisors fitting closely over the lower (scissor bite). Lips tight and clean.

NECK Medium length, refined and slightly crested, fitting gracefully into the shoulders. Well covered with long silky hair.

FOREQUARTERS Shoulders fine and well laid back, fitting with well-angulated upper arms snugly to the ribs. Elbows turned neither in nor out. The forelegs have refined, round bones and are straight and set well under the body, with no weakness in the pasterns.

BODY This should be moderately long in proportion to the height of the dog. Level topline, well sprung ribs extending back to strong loins. Chest of moderate depth and breadth. A topline showing a roach or dip is a serious fault.

HINDQUARTERS The thighs must be well developed and the stifles should be well turned and the hocks well bent. When viewed from behind, the hocks should be well let down and parallel with each other.

FEET Small, well padded, cat-like, with closely knit toes; the toe nails must be black or very dark.

TAIL Preferably docked, set on high and carried erect but not over-gay. Should be free of feathering.

GAIT/MOVEMENT The movement should be free and true without slackness at elbows or shoulders, there should be no turning in nor out of the feet or pasterns. The hindquarters should have strong propelling power with ample flexibility at stifles and hocks. Viewed from behind the movement should be neither too close nor too wide.

COAT Must be flat, fine and glossy and of a silky texture with a length of coat from 13 to 15 cms (5 to 6 ins) from behind the ears to the set on of the tail, but must not impede the dog's action. The legs from knees and hocks to feet free from long hair.

COLOUR Blue and tan or grey-blue and tan, the richer the better. Blue on the tail to be very dark. Silver blue or fawn topknot desirable. Distribution of blue and tan as follows: tan around the base of the ears, muzzle, and on the sides of the cheeks; blue from the base of the skull to the tip of tail, running down the fore-legs to near the knees and down the thighs to the hocks; tan line showing down the stifles and from the knees and hocks to the toes and around the vent. The body colour must be free from smut or dark shading. Black colouring is permissible in puppies. Blue colour must be established by 18 months of age.

SIZE Height: Dogs approx. 23 cms (9 ins) at the withers. Bitches slightly less. Weight: Desirable weight from 3.5 to 4.5 kgs (approximately 8 to 10 lbs).

FAULTS Any departure from the foregoing points should be considered a fault and the seriousness with which the fault should be regarded should be in exact proportion to its degree.

NOTE Male animals should have two apparently normal testicles fully descended into the scrotum.

Standard issued by the Australian National Kennel Council.

THE BRITISH BREED STANDARD

As his name implies, this dog originated in Australia and, at one time, was known as the 'Sydney Silky'. Although he is in the Toy Group, he is far from being a quiet little lap dog. His background comes from a mixture of Australian and Yorkshire Terriers, and he retains many of the qualities of these breeds. He is friendly but independent, smart and curious, energetic, affectionate, and has lots of stamina. Primarily he was bred to be a household pet, and he fills this role admirably. His glossy, silky coat, which is five or six inches long, is easy to look after and a few minutes daily brushing, with a quick comb and parting down the back, gives him a well groomed appearance.

GENERAL APPEARANCE Compact, moderately low-set, medium length with refined structure; sufficient substance to suggest ability to hunt and kill domestic rodents. Straight silky hair parted from nape of neck to root of tail, presenting a well groomed appearance.

CHARACTERISTICS Terrier-like, keen, alert, active.

TEMPERAMENT Very friendly, quick and responsive.

HEAD AND SKULL Moderate length, slightly shorter in length from tip of nose to between eyes than from there to top rear of occiput. Moderately broad between ears; skull flat, without fullness between eyes. Nose black.

EYES Small, round, dark as possible, not prominent, keen intelligent expression.

EARS Small, V-shaped, with fine leathers, high on skull and pricked; entirely free from long hair.

MOUTH Jaws strong, with a perfect, regular and complete scissor bite, i.e. upper teeth closely overlapping lower teeth and set square to the jaws. Teeth even and not cramped, lips tight and clean.

NECK Medium length, refined, slightly arched. Well covered with long silky hair.

FOREQUARTERS Shoulders fine, well laid back, well angulated upper arms fitting snugly to ribs; elbows turn neither in nor out; forelegs straight with refined round bone, set well under body with no weakness in pasterns.

BODY Slightly longer than height. Level top-line; well sprung ribs extending back to strong loins. Chest of moderate depth and breadth.

HINDQUARTERS Thighs well developed. Stifles well turned; when viewed from behind, the hocks well let down and parallel.

FEET Small, well padded and cat-like. Closely knit toes with black or very dark toenails.

TAIL Customarily docked, carried erect; not over-gay; free from feathering.

GAIT/MOVEMENT Free, straight forward without slackness at shoulders or elbows. No turning sideways of feet or pasterns. Hindquarters have strong propelling power with ample flexibility at stifles and hocks. Viewed from behind, movement neither too close nor too wide.

COAT Straight, fine and glossy; silky texture; length of coat 13 to 15 cms (5 to 6 ins) from behind ears to set-on of tail desirable. Legs, from knees and hocks to feet, free of long hair. Fine silky 'top-knot', not falling over eyes. Long fall of hair on foreface and cheeks undesirable.

COLOUR Blue and tan, grey-blue and tan, the richer these colours the better. Blue on tail very dark. Distribution of blue and tan as follows: silver-blue or fawn top-knot, tan around base of ears, muzzle, and on side of cheeks; blue from base of skull to tip of tail, running down forelegs to near knees and down thighs to hocks; tan line showing down stifles, and tan from knees and hocks to toes and around vent. Blue colour must be established by 18 months of age.

SIZE Most desirable weight about 4 kgs (8 to 10 lbs). Height approximately 23 cms (9 ins) at withers, bitches may be slightly less.

FAULTS Any departure from the foregoing points should be considered a fault and the seriousness with which the fault should be regarded should be in exact proportion to its degree.

NOTE Male animals should have two apparently normal testicles fully descended into the scrotum.

Reproduced by kind permission of the Kennel Club.

THE AMERICAN BREED STANDARD

CHANGES TO THE AMERICAN BREED STANDARD, 1989
The official 1959 AKC Standard for the

breed was changed, effective from November 30th 1989, to bring it more in line with the official Australian Standard. A list of the major changes in the new Standard follows. The size description changed from including a weight range of 8 to 10 lbs and shoulder height of 9 to 10 inches. The weight requirement was dropped entirely but the height requirement stayed the same. The back line is change from being described as straight with a just perceptible rounding over the loin, to level. Roaching or dipping are now considered a serious fault. The tail-set was described as set high and erect, or semi-erect but not over-gay. It is now described as set high and carried at the twelve to two o'clock position. Angulation of the hindquarters changed from moderate to well-angulated at the stifles. Coat is now described as straight, single, glossy and silky in texture. On matured specimens the coat falls below and follows the body outline, rather than being described as flat, fine, glossy and silky. It no longer requires a desired length of from five to six inches from behind the ears to the set-on of the tail. The colour requirements, temperament and movement remain the same.

GENERAL APPEARANCE The Silky Terrier is a true "toy terrier". He is moderately low set, slightly longer than tall, of refined bone structure, but of sufficient substance to suggest the ability to hunt and kill domestic rodents. His coat is silky in texture, parted from the stop to the tail and presents a well groomed but not sculptured appearance. His inquisitive nature and joy of life make him an ideal companion.

SIZE, PROPORTION, SUBSTANCE *Size* Shoulder height from nine to ten inches. Deviation in either direction is undesirable. *Proportion* The body is about one fifth longer than the dog's height at the withers. *Substance* Lightly built with strong but rather fine bone.

HEAD The head is strong, wedge-shaped, and moderately long. *Expression* piercingly keen. *Eyes* small, dark, almond-shaped with dark rims. Light eyes are a serious fault. *Ears* are small, V-shaped, set high and carried erect without any tendency to flare obliquely off the skull. *Skull* flat, and not too wide between the ears. The skull is slightly longer than the muzzle. *Stop* shallow. The *nose* is black. *Teeth* strong and well aligned, scissors bite. An undershot or overshot bite is a serious fault.

NECK, TOPLINE, BODY The *neck* fits gracefully into sloping shoulders. It is medium-long, fine, and to some degree crested. The *topline* is level. A topline showing a roach or dip is a serious fault. *Chest* medium wide and deep enough to extend down to the elbows. The *body* is moderately low set and about one-fifth longer than the dog's height at the withers. The body is measured from the point of the shoulder (or forechest) to the rearmost projection of the upper thigh (or point of the buttocks). A body which is too short is a fault, as is a body which is too long. The *tail* is docked, set high and carried at twelve to two o'clock position.

FOREQUARTERS Well laid back shoulders, together with proper angulation at the upper arm, set the forelegs nicely under the body. Forelegs are strong, straight and rather fine-boned. *Feet* small, catlike, round, compact. Pads are thick and springy while nails are strong and dark-colored. White or flesh-colored nails are a fault. The feet point straight ahead, with no turning in or out. Dewclaws, if any, are removed.

HINDQUARTERS Thighs well muscled and strong, but not so developed as to appear heavy. Well angulated stifles with low hocks which are parallel when viewed from behind. *Feet* as in front.

COAT Straight, single, glossy, silky in texture. On matured specimens the coat falls below and follows the body outline. It should not approach floor length. On the top of the head, the hair is so profuse as to form a topknot, but long hair on the face and ears is objectionable. The hair is parted on the head and down over the back to the root of the tail. The tail is well coated but devoid of plume. Legs should have short hair from the pastern and hock joints to the feet. The feet should not be obscured by the leg furnishings.

COLOR Blue and tan. The blue may be silver blue, pigeon blue or slate blue, the tan deep and rich. The blue extends from the base of the skull to the tip of the tail, down the forelegs to the elbows, and half way down the outside of the thighs. On the tail the blue should be very dark. Tan appears on muzzle and cheeks, around the base of the ears, on the legs and feet and around the vent. The topknot should be silver or fawn which is lighter than the tan points.

GAIT Should be free, light-footed, lively and straight forward. Hindquarters should have strong propelling power. Toeing in or out is to be faulted.

TEMPERAMENT The keenly alert air of the terrier is characteristic, with shyness or excessive nervousness to be faulted. The manner is quick, friendly, responsive.

Reproduced by kind permission of the American Kennel Club
(Approved October 10, 1989)

THE FINER POINTS OF THE SILKY STANDARDS

We often forget that the Silky Terrier is a comparatively 'new' breed of dog and so we are bound to produce different types within our litters until we have sufficient blood lines to breed to type. It is important that those engaged in breeding the Silky recognise the correct type, as set down in the Standard, before they go any further. Anyone can breed litter after litter, but what is important is that each litter should and must be superior to the last.

GENERAL APPEARANCE

One must aim for a glamorous dog, of the correct colour and, most of all, typical of its breed. Originally the Silky was bred to work as a hunter and killer of domestic rodents and must, therefore, show no signs of weediness or nervousness, but should give an impression of agility and speed, plus having the stamina to work. The key words relevant to the overall Silky are "moderate", "medium" and "refined" in relation to structure and appearance. The dog should have no look of legginess or wiriness about the frame, yet while compact, should in no way be coarse or gross, as it is most essential to retain the refinement asked for.

THE HEAD
When looking at a Silky, the dog should always be balanced. Again the word moderate is used, with no exaggeration

HEAD PROPORTIONS

LEFT: Correct head proportions.

BOTTOM LEFT: Incorrect. Muzzle too short.

BOTTOM RIGHT: Incorrect: Muzzle too long.

THE EARS

Correct: Small, V-shaped, set high and carried erect.

Incorrect: Set too low, flaring obliquely from the skull.

Incorrect: Rounded, too big.

Incorrect: 'Leaf ear'.

necessary. The head should be of moderate length, from the occiput to the stop being slightly longer than from stop to nose, i.e. three parts skull, two parts muzzle. The head should not be so large as to require a large, heavy body; it should be Terrier-like. The head tapers more than that of the Yorkshire Terrier, but the muzzle must not be so snipy as to cause cramped or missing teeth. When handling the skull, it should be flat, and there must be no fullness between the eyes. The stop is less than that of the Yorkie. While it is very objectionable for the length of hair on the cheeks to be "long", it is necessary to have some length of hair on cheeks and foreface, but short, compared to that of the surrounding head and neck fall. There should be a fine silky topknot, not falling over the eyes. This is more a matter of correct grooming, as it is not common for well-coated dogs to have the topknot falling naturally only to the sides of the head.

THE EARS
The ears should be small, V-shaped and pricked. They should be set high on the head. They should be carried entirely perpendicular to the plane of the head. Ears that are too large, or are round-pointed, or set low on the head, or ears that flare out to the sides, completely spoil an otherwise correct picture.

THE EYES
The eyes are of great importance in making for a correct head. They should be small, round, dark in colour, placed neither too far apart nor too close together and showing a keen intelligent expression. They are inclined to be set a little more to the sides of the head rather than looking straight ahead. Almost circular, or round,

probably describes the ideal shape. Eye rims should be black or dark brown. The beady black eyes required in some Terriers are not correct for the Silky, as they do not denote the keen intelligence required.

THE NOSE
The nose should be black. Silkies do not generally suffer from 'winter noses' – that is when pigment is lost during the winter months and the nose turns pink.

THE MOUTH
The mouth must be strong, with strong teeth which are evenly spaced, not cramped. A scissor bite is called for, that is when the top teeth closely overlap the bottom teeth. Lips should be clean. Watch for missing incisors, most commonly of the bottom jaw.

THE NECK
The neck should be of medium length with a slight crest. It must not be thick set. A Silky would look more graceful with a neck which was slightly longer, than with a short neck. A slight crest is required, to add refinement and grace.

THE FOREQUARTERS
The forequarters should be fine and well laid back, with well-angulated upper arms fitting snugly to the ribs. Elbows should be turned neither in nor out. The forelegs should have refined, round bone, and be set well under the body. There should be no weakness in the pasterns. Silkies are usually congratulated on how muscular they are. Once again, 'fine' shoulders and 'refined' round bone are specified. The set of the forelegs could not be more clearly described. Unfortunately fronts are a failing in Silkies, those having 'straight' fronts

BODY LENGTH

Correct body length.

Incorrect: Too short.

Incorrect: Too long.

often being straight in shoulder also. There are some exceptionally good fronts, but they are few and far between.

THE BODY

The body length appears to be slightly longer from the shoulders to the tail set than it is in height. Moderate depth and breadth of chest is required. The top-line can best be judged with the dog on the move. It should be straight. Roached backs, short backs, dipping at the shoulders, and a too long back (although in bitches this is sometimes accepted) are faults and should be avoided. With a dog that measures 10 inches at the shoulders, the length from the withers to the tail would be 12 inches for ideal proportions.

THE HINDQUARTERS

The hindquarters must have the thighs well-developed. The stifles should be well turned with hocks well let down and parallel with each other when viewed from behind.

THE FEET

The feet are small, well-padded and cat-like with closely knit toes. Front feet should point forwards, not ten past two or fiddle-shaped. Toe nails must be black or very dark.

THE TAIL

The tail is customarily docked when the puppy is only a few days old, although now we can find Silkies carrying a full flag. The

TAIL-SET

Correct tail-set.

Incorrect: Too gay.

Incorrect: Too low-set.

TAIL DOCK

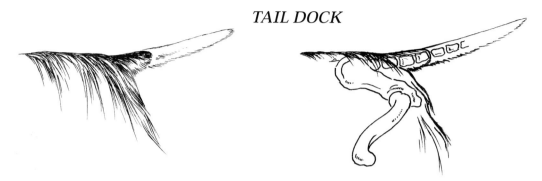

The tail is customarily docked, although in some countries the Silky carries a full flag.

tail should be set on high and carried straight up, not gay and never lower than ten past. It should be covered in coat which is darker in blue than that of the body coat. It should not be trimmed as short as on feet and muzzle. With a full tail, the coat could be graduated in length from the base to the tip. A tail which is "over-gay" i.e. one which almost lies on the top of the back, is undesirable. Most Silky people prefer a slightly gay tail rather than a tail carried only level with the back, especially while on the move.

THE COAT

The coat must be straight, of true silky texture, glossy and gleaming with quality. It should hang flat to the sides of the body, and it has no undercoat. The length of the coat is approximately five inches and this is lying in layers from the central parting. Daylight should be seen under the coat. It should follow the contour of the underbody, never straight, nor touching the ground, as it does with a Yorkshire Terrier. It is possible to have a floor-length coat on a young dog at one year of age. Usually this would be found on a wrong-textured coat.

Aust. Ch. Kelbrae Rhubarb displaying a good length of coat which does not impede movement.

Silkies which have taken some time to grow coat usually have the better coat. If the coat is too profuse, it will not hang flat. Too much coat is also faulty and would resemble the woolly coat often found in the Yorkshire Terrier. Legs and feet to be free from *long* hair (13 to 15 cms). This does not necessarily mean that they should be trimmed extremely close to the skin.

COLOUR

There is a great deal of confusion as to what shades of blue are correct. The American Standard calls for silver blue, pigeon blue or slate blue. The colours overlap, which reads as though any stage of blue is correct. A coat which is blue will be seen at the roots to be quite dark. This would be seen down the parting. The almost white coat is not correct. A good colour will carry a blue cast at all times. Some body coats tend towards grey rather than blue, but since grey-blue is a shade of the blue colour, the grey-blue should not be faulted. The blue on the tail has to be darker than that on the body. A silver blue or fawn topknot is desirable. The forehead coat should always be lighter than that on the chest and legs.

The distribution of the tan should be as follows: tan around the base of the ears, muzzle and on the sides of the cheeks; blue from the base of the skull to the tip of the tail, running down the forelegs to near the knees and down the thighs to the hocks; tan line showing down the stifles and from the knees and hocks to the toes and around the vent. The body coat must be free from sooty or dark shading. Black/dark blue colouring is permissible in puppies but the blue body coat must be established by 18 months. A black/dark saddle of coarser coat across the back of an adult dog is undesirable. Coat colour, whichever colour of blue it is, must not carry a bronze cast. When judging the Silky, preference should be given to the rich blue, with rich tan points and a silver/blue or fawn topknot, but soundness should take overall preference. To colour judge Silkies is wrong; type and soundness must be strongly considered.

GAIT/MOVEMENT

On the move the Silky is free, lightfooted, very lively and buoyant (the more cat-like the better) but at one with the dog's handler. Movement should be true coming and going, with good drive from the hindquarters. A Silky which plods round the ring is not typical of the breed. Cow-hocks or very close movement behind are serious faults, as is weaving of the front legs. This is when one leg comes over the plane of the other leg (twisting). When very intent on some object, a Silky will often raise one front foot in the air and hold it there, much like a pointer. Some Silkies will also do this when stopped during gaiting around the ring. This should never be faulted in the show ring as it is characteristic of the breed.

6 THE SHOW SILKY

You might ask – why should I show my dog? The answer is that you will have the opportunity to achieve satisfaction and enjoyment: satisfaction in the knowledge that you have chosen a hobby whereby the entire family can spend time together; enjoyment by having the opportunity to meet fellow exhibitors and cement new friendships in your own country or overseas, and also learn more about this wonderful little dog, the Australian Silky Terrier. Having acquired your first Australian Silky, and with the help of the breeder, and fellow exhibitors, you have decided that you might like to show your young puppy.

Now that you are ready to show your Australian Silky, you will find that there are social advantages to be obtained by attending special training classes, where you can learn what is expected of you and your dog or bitch on the big day. You will have the chance to meet other new exhibitors, just like yourself, with a common interest, and apprehension, about entering the ring with your puppy. Also there will, in most countries, be a breed club, which you can join. Nearly all clubs publish a magazine or newsletter, which enables you to keep abreast of forthcoming functions, and gives helpful information about dogs in general.

It is important you attend some kind of training classes with your puppy before you enter and exhibit at a show. Contact your local Dog Society to find out if they hold such an event, and if so, when and where. By attending some kind of training, you will feel a lot more confident when the time comes for you to enter the ring. This confidence will also transmit down the lead to your puppy, and both of you will find that you enjoy your day a lot more. When you achieve your first success in the show ring, you will be rewarded a hundredfold – knowing that you have mastered the art of showing, and that all your hard work has paid off.

However, there is another facet of dog shows, and that is the ability to accept a judge's decisions, and this becomes a test of one's character; and there is also the ability to stay calm if you do not win, and this is a test of one's temperament. One might ask, why would I want to put myself in that situation? The answer is simple: it is a way of teaching oneself to be a much better person. After all, you must always remember that it is a hobby, and if one had a perfect dog and the judges placed that dog first every time, where would the enjoyment be in going along to a dog show each weekend in the knowledge that the same dog was going to win? Even if there was a perfect dog, everybody has their own opinion, and the judge on the day might not agree that it is so, and then it becomes the judge's decision, which is the reason why we exhibit again next time, in the hope that the judge might consider our dog to be the winner. Basically, this is why we show our dog.

By choosing an Australian Silky, you have chosen a breed which is by nature a Terrier, so these are strong, active little dogs to handle. They are also a relatively easy dog to groom and prepare for show day, with a minimal amount of trimming necessary for the purpose of exhibiting. You will also learn that they very quickly become accustomed to attending shows, and they get to know that bath time means show time.

ASSESSING A POTENTIAL SHOW DOG

When you purchased your Silky, the breeder may have referred to the puppy as being of 'show potential'. This means that the puppy has, at that moment, all the indications of becoming a show dog. But during the puppy's growth, and as the milk teeth are replaced with permanent teeth, and the dark body coat changes colour, a lot can happen. The coat will break from a dark blue/black to a rich steel blue grey. The average Silky does not usually develop an adult colour until at least eighteen months of age. It is very difficult to assess the potential of a 10 to 12-week-old puppy. That is why, if you intend to show your Silky, you should be looking for the best

you can buy and the puppy should, preferably, be from a sire and dam who have been exhibited in a serious manner, and whom you have seen.

Before assessing a potential show dog, you should first obtain and read the approved and adopted Standard of the Silky Terrier, from the Kennel Club or Breed Society Secretary. To help you understand the Standard in relation to assessing the potential show dog, this section is divided into two sections, a *puppy* and a *mature* dog. The following is a guide for you to follow.

Puppies' heads should be typy – with small V-shaped ears set high. Very young puppies' ears will still be fallen. However, by holding the ear erect with your hand, you will be able to gauge the size of the ear, and the ear placement. Puppies with large low-set ears are likely to have pendant ears. The puppies' eyes must be dark; avoid puppies with light eyes – they will not darken with age. Also, a prominent eye is to be avoided, as it will become more prominent as the puppy matures. The muzzle of the puppy should not be overly long, as the Standard says 'slightly shorter from tip of the nose to between the eyes than from the same position to the occiput (back of skull)'. Remember also that the muzzle will lengthen as the puppy gains adult teeth. The puppy's bite must be correct: a scissor bite is what is required – that is, top teeth fitting just over bottom teeth. A bad bite, either undershot (bottom teeth in front of top) or overshot (top teeth too far over the bottom), will mean a bad bite in a mature dog.

When assessing a potential mature show dog, the head is a very important part of the dog. Reading the Standard, it is fairly self-explanatory, except that no mention is

Aust. Ch. Kelbrae Rubarb, pictured at six months of age, showing the typical head of a young dog.

made of the fact that they must have a slight stop at the base of the nose between the eyes. If there is no stop the head is completely wrong. Length of muzzle is important, as explained above with regard to a puppy. Eyes should be small, round and as dark as possible. Strong jaws with a scissor bite are required, once again as explained above.

Look for a good length of neck. A puppy who always carries the head down when moving will either be stuffy-necked (neck too short) or have an incorrect front assembly. In some cases the puppy could have both. In an adult dog, a dog with a medium length of neck, well-muscled, is a sign of the terrier's ability.

The puppy's shoulder blade must be of good length, with about a 90 degree angle of upper arm to shoulder blade, with upper arm and shoulder blade about the same length. Front legs must be well set under the puppy's body. An adult Australian Silky with the correct neck generally means that the forequarters will be correct, and elbows will turn neither in nor out. Remember, the bone is to be refined and round. Substance of bone is required without coarseness; bone that is too fine usually results in a weak action. Strong pasterns are essential.

ABOVE: Aust. NZ Ch. Tarawera My Steel Dan: A dog with well-sprung ribs and a good depth of chest. The back extends to strong loins.

LEFT: The mature dog: Aust. Ch. Tarawera Pippin showing a head of medium length, with a refined and slightly crested neck.

A puppy's chest should extend down to the elbows. Ribs must be well sprung (plenty of chest room) and well ribbed back. Ribs that extend back beyond the half-way point of the body usually indicate a good level topline. This also can be said of a good tail-set. A puppy with a low tail-set is likely to have a bad topline. The body width of a young puppy at eight to ten weeks should be the same in the hindquarters as in the front assembly.

In a mature dog, look for a dog that is oblong, bearing in mind that the Standard calls for a dog of 23 cms (approximately nine inches), although in practice the majority of dogs today are in the 25 to 27 cms (approximately ten to ten-and-a-half inch) bracket. One does not want a square dog, which is more to the Yorkshire Terrier type, and with an overly long-bodied dog you will find either sway or roach backs. Ideally the ratio is 1 to 1.25, so if you have a 23 cms (9 inch) dog, its length would be approximately 29.5 cms (eleven and a half inches) – this length is from withers to tail-set. A level topline while the dog is on the move and when the dog is standing is essential. Well-sprung ribs give plenty of chest capacity, extending back to strong loins and strong muscles, which give strength and agility.

A puppy from eight weeks with cow-hocks is not likely to improve. Here again, a mature dog with cow hocks, or anything that is not parallel, is not acceptable. You are looking for hocks that are well let down, not long. In puppies and mature dogs, the feet are required to be small, catlike, with closely knit toes with black or very dark toenails. The impression left by a compact cat foot is round, not oval.

If a puppy has a correct neck (carrying the head held high, not down), and forequarters, you will have correct movement. Correct hindquarters will, as the dog matures, have strong propelling power. Looking at a mature dog, the movement is very proud, head held high,

Tarawera Catriona: A typical Silky at six months of age.

free and straight forward. They should have hindquarters with strong propelling power, and when viewed from behind, the movement should be neither too close nor too wide. They are a very active and agile dog, and correct drive from the hindquarters will enable them to go all day.

In both puppies and adult dogs the tail should be docked and carried erect. This is self-explanatory: we do not want to see a tail that is over the back (over-gay), nor one that is carried as low as a Yorkshire Terrier. Silkies' tails should always be carried erect on the move and while standing, not jammed down between their back legs, although sometimes when exhibiting, if it is a hot day, their tail will not be as erect as one would like. If puppies have their tails down, not erect, this usually means that a temperament problem exists.

When assessing a puppy's coat, it must be fine and silky to the touch, hence Silky Terrier. Avoid a puppy with a thick woolly coat. In a mature Silky Terrier, it is that word 'Silky', which sets them apart from the Australian Terrier. Length of coat is

where they differ from the Yorkshire Terrier, and this should be from 13 to 15 cms (five to six inches) from behind the ears to the set-on of the tail, and must not impede the dog's action. This does not mean that you should have 13 to 15 cms of coat from under the stomach. If you have, say, a 23 to 25 cms dog, measured at the withers (the highest part of the back behind the shoulders) and with the correct length of coat, you will be able to see the dog's feet and a certain amount of daylight under the dog. They are a well-muscled little dog bred for a purpose, to be a 'Terrier', not a dog to be sitting on your lap or lounging about all day, and a long coat sweeping the ground is highly undesirable.

A puppy's colour must be black and tan, with blue colour on body being established by 18 months of age. In young puppies up to, say, 12 months of age you will most likely find them having a 'Silver-Blue' topknot, but unfortunately, as they mature, this becomes, in most cases, 'Fawn'. The body colour of a mature dog has been a bone of contention for many years. You hear some of the older breeders saying they prefer the light-coloured ones. It all comes down to the fact that the Standard states 'Blue and Tan, or Grey Blue and Tan, the richer of these colours the better'. People attempting to visualise the colour of an Australian Silky have over the years asked me to describe the colour to them, and my only answer is that very important word '*blue*'. Grey-Blue does not mean 'silver or nearly white', and Blue does not mean the 'Dark Steel Blue' of a Yorkshire Terrier. Tan, just as you would imagine this to be, is not a light fawn colour. Tan should be around the base of the ears, muzzle and sides of cheeks, with a tan line showing down the stifles and from the knees and hocks to the toes and around the vent. The topknot is Silver Blue or Fawn. Always bear in mind that an Australian Silky Terrier is a three-coloured dog, with each colour being designated to a certain part of the dog.

SHOW TRAINING

Now you have your new little puppy, it is time to start show training. Because this is a youngster, do not be too hard on the little dog, as we want this experience to be enjoyed, otherwise the puppy will not enjoy showing. Commence your training with approximately five-minute sessions and increase gradually. Eventually, do not let show training last longer than 15 minutes a day. Always master one exercise at a time; do not crowd the puppy's mind with two or three different exercises at one time – remember they are intelligent but their concentration span is not great. If the trainer is becoming irritable, do not continue; cease training and try again the next day. Do not forget the most important part of training: always finish with a play session.

LEARNING THE STAND

Keep this exercise fairly simple. Stand your puppy with four feet placed firmly on your grooming table, encouraging the puppy to keep both head and tail up. At the same time, while you are doing this, talk to your puppy by saying "Stand – good boy" or "good girl" and tickling your Silky gently under the chin. After a while it is a good idea to use different surfaces while performing this exercise, because your puppy will have to become accustomed to standing on a variety of surfaces and tables at the shows. Always, when you are doing this, make sure that the surface is firm; you do not want your puppy to be frightened by having a bad experience on an insecure surface. Now that your puppy has mastered the Stand on the table, it is time to start training for the hands on. Commence by looking into your puppy's mouth. Some days the puppy will not want you to do this, as there will be times when the teeth and gums are sore, and this will be during teething. Praise the puppy when you are allowed to inspect the teeth. Also, while your puppy is standing on the table, run your hands down the puppy's front, over the body and down the hindquarters. If it is a male, gently place your hand between his back legs as if to check that he is entire. If this is done every time you have your puppy on the table, then the puppy will not object to being handled by judges during examinations for conformation at shows.

The next phase of learning the Stand is on the ground. It is a good idea to get hold of a mirror and stand it upright on the ground and teach your puppy to stand in front of it. In this way you will be able to see what your puppy looks like from the judge's position and decide whether the topline is level, or whether the puppy's hindquarters need to be placed square etc. I like to see a Silky free-standing, which means walking them into a position and then standing. It is a good idea to train them so that they will let you touch them on the ground, in case you need to correct their fronts or re-set their hindquarters. This will only be achieved by practising at home. Once you have them standing on the ground, the next step is to introduce them to a bait, or, if you wish to, call it a treat. Place the food in your pocket and teach the dog to be alert to the fact that you have it there and tempt the puppy with it for a short time. Always remember to give the puppy a piece once an exercise has been performed to your satisfaction, and only then. Never put a piece of food in the dog's mouth when a judge is handling the dog. And, always remember, praise and play at the end of each session.

LEAD TRAINING

In most cases the first time on a lead meets with some resistance: be patient to help overcome the puppy's anxiety and fear. As mentioned previously, a small collar left on for a short time each day will help your puppy become accustomed to having something around the neck. Use a buckle-type collar that can be fitted so that it is not too tight, and not loose enough that it can be pulled over the head, or a paw get caught in it. Do not let your puppy become distressed with the collar on at any time; if this happens remove it and try again the next day. Attach a lead to the collar and, while supervising, let the puppy run around with the lead attached to the collar for a short time each day. The next step is to encourage the puppy to trot along with you. At first you will strike some resistance, the puppy will go in all directions, and

Aust. Ch. Dulcannina Jodi Knight: This dog poses well, due to good training from puppyhood. The key to successful show training is to keep the sessions short, and always end on a positive note.

jump and pull. Let this continue for a short time until the puppy's initial burst of energy has subsided, then entice the puppy to go with you by talking, coaxing with maybe some small piece of food, or with one of the pup's squeaky toys.

Always make sure that the puppy walks on your left hand side, as this is what is required when exhibiting your puppy at a show. Never, at any stage, pull the puppy along, as this will destroy what you are trying to achieve as your puppy will immediately have the sensation of choking. You will always get a rebel puppy who just digs their heels in, and in this case it will need just patience and perseverance by the person training the puppy, but believe me your puppy will eventually trot alongside you. If you have a rebellious puppy, put the lead on and hold it loosely in your left hand; in your right hand have a small piece of biscuit (or the like) and, holding this in front of the puppy's head, walk slowly. The puppy will gradually learn to move alongside you, aware of the lead, but head up looking for the treat that you are holding up in front. At short intervals let the puppy have a reward, and always use an appropriate word at this time – Walk, Steady, etc. Gradually lengthen the time between rewards while carrying out this exercise, but continue to encourage and praise. Once you have mastered the art of lead training, practise moving the puppy in a triangle or straight up and back, finally coming to a stop and standing as still as possible with the puppy looking up – at this point you can use the exercise of having a tempting tidbit in your pocket.

All of the above will take time and patience. Always finish each training session with play, and never lose your cool, because if you do all your previous hard work will be lost. Start showing with the light flat show leads; the most popular seem to be those that have the lead and collar all in one, with a sliding loop and ring that expands or contracts the collar size to suit the different size dogs. These light leads do not detract from the dog while showing. Only use these lightweight leads when showing and in your own backyard; do not exercise your puppy outside your premises on this type of lead. For security reasons, use a collar and separate lead which attaches to the collar.

LEARNING THE TURN

Learning the turn is one of the most important moves to practise. There are a number of ways to turn, and it is necessary not to break the dog's rhythm or gait, so try and make these turns as smooth as possible. In fact, this is the time to look about for local training clubs who specialise in show training, not obedience training. It is not good to train for show and obedience at the same time, as this will only confuse your Silky – you will want your dog to stand in the show ring when you stop walking, not to sit, as is required in obedience.

At your first visit to a training session just sit and watch, so that both you and your puppy take in what is going on. If the training sessions are at an All Breed Club then your puppy will have to get used to being with large dogs. The training sessions can take the form of a 'Match' where handlers all have a number. Two numbers are called out at random and the dogs are judged, one against the other. The winner goes on to meet another dog or puppy in a later round. Unfortunately the dog who is knocked out in the first round does not experience much training!

The other type of training is run on similar lines to a 'mini-show'. Dogs or puppies are entered in classes, usually grouped by age, and you can enter as many as you like. These sessions are an ideal way for you to learn how to show dogs. Watch the more experienced handlers and dogs, and learn. When your class number is called out by the steward you take your pup into the ring. You will be required to stand with your pup on a lead. As standing still is not something puppies really want to do, you may have to crouch down and encourage your Silky to do what is required. The puppies will be asked to stand, and the judge will examine them. You will have to walk your puppy up and down while the judge assesses each dog against the others in the class. Small dogs are assessed on a table and are required to stand still while the judge runs his hands over, feeling the conformation of the dog. You will then be asked to walk your dog.

Remember that you should have your dog on your lefthand side when walking. At the end of the walk-way you turn together. Walk round your pup, do not let your pup walk round you, otherwise the puppy will have gone ahead of you and you will have broken the rhythm. At all times the handler must not come between the judge and the dog. Use some form of instruction at the turn. Many handlers tell their dog to 'turn'. If you are having trouble keeping your dog's attention, talk, give praise, use a tasty tidbit.

ENTERING YOUR FIRST SHOW

You now have your Silky Terrier trained and ready to commence showing. Today most countries have a governing body, which controls activities regarding conformation showing, Obedience trials and match events. Your first step in showing your Australian Silky would be to contact your respective controlling body, so that you can find out what is required with regard to membership and eligibility. Official show entry forms are available from your controlling body, which you are required to fill in and post to the show secretary prior to the shows. Once you have fulfilled the requirements of your controlling body, it is now up to you to decide which event you wish to enter. Most countries have either Open Shows or Match shows which are good training events for you and your dog. These shows may also be events where judges are also

being trained.

The other type of show is what is called a Championship Show, where championship points are awarded. Each country has different qualifications that are required in order for your dog to gain a Championship title. Once again, your controlling body will be able to supply you with this information. At first it is a good idea to enter an Open Show or a Match Event, which are a good training ground for your first show, and also most puppies are nervous at their first show, so if they do not perform as expected all is not lost. There is a closing date for entries for each show, after which the Show Secretary cannot accept further entries, so be sure to mail the completed official entry form, duly completed with the correct information, together with cheque or money order for entry fee, in plenty of time. Some shows require you to send a stamped self-addressed envelope for the return of exhibit numbers, and other shows require you to pick up your numbers on the morning of the show.

SHOWS IN THE USA

There are two major types of dog shows, Specialty and all-breed shows; there are also Match Shows, which are usually judged by those who are aspiring to become Championship Show judges. Classes usually range from Puppy through Novice and Post-graduate to Open. Champions are not eligible for Matches. The Specialty shows are limited to dogs of a specific breed. All-breed shows are open to over one hundred and thirty breeds recognised by the AKC. The actual system of showing is far different from the system in the UK, although the final aim is the same – to make your dog into a Champion, carry on to go Best of Breed and maybe even Best in Show. Most of the dogs in shows are seeking to win points towards their title of Champion. This means that the dog must win fifteen points including two 'majors'. A 'major' is a win of three, four or five points. These points must be won under at least three different judges. A dog can win from one to five points, according to the number of dogs competing in each breed. There are usually six regular classes in which a dog can be entered: Puppy, Twelve to Eighteen Months, Novice, Bred by Exhibitor, American-Bred, and Open.

After these six classes are judged, the class winners compete for best of the first place dogs. This is done for each sex. Only the Winners Dog and the Winners Bitch receive Championship points. (A Reserve Winner award is given to the runner-up in each sex.) At this point, the Winners Dog and the Winners Bitch compete with the Champions for Best of Breed.

At the end of the BOB judging, three awards are usually given: Best of Breed – the dog judged as the best in its breed category; Best of Winners – the dog judged as best between Winners Dog and Winners Bitch; and Best of Opposite Sex – the dog that is the opposite sex of the BOB winner.

Each BOB winner goes forward to compete in one of the seven Groups. There are four placings in every Group but only the first in each Group goes forward to compete for the Best in Show. There are two very interesting points here. An up-and-coming dog can become a Champion without having to compete against other Champions. The necessary points are won before they come up against the Champions, although additional points may be earned if the class dog defeats a Champion. Championship points are

The American show scene: Am. Int. Ch. Tawny Mist Touch of Excitement (Am. Ch. Marina's Houston ROMX – Am. Ch. Tawny Mist Touch of Class ROMX): A multiple Group-placing Silky.

Ashbey Photography.

awarded according to the number of dogs which are present at the show. The more dogs present and beaten, the higher the number of points awarded – five being the top number. In conclusion, once the status of Champion has been achieved, the dog can compete for BOB without having to win in the other classes.

SHOWS IN THE UK
The UK has a slightly different system for

The British show scene: Sonia Saxby pictured with Call Me Sydney.

showing from that obtaining in other countries. And it has to be remembered that the Australian Silky has not, as yet, been awarded Challenge Certificates, therefore no matter how often a dog wins top awards, Champion status cannot be granted. Nevertheless, Silkies are being exhibited at all types of shows. Dogs must be six months old before they can be entered for a show, and only entered dogs may be present at dog shows.

At Sanction or Primary Shows entries are made on the day and classes are for pedigree dogs and non-pedigree dogs. This type of show is usually held to raise funds for a charity. It is a fun day out and

generally includes classes such as 'The dog the Judge would like to take home' and 'The dog with the waggiest tail'!

Limited Shows are held for members of that particular Society or Club. You must be a member to enter these shows. Classification is of a more general nature – Any Variety Toy, Any Variety Gundog etc.

Open Shows are held by Societies and Clubs. They are held once or twice a year. Anyone can enter their dog provided that the dog is Kennel Club registered. If it is a general society then all breeds of dogs are eligible to enter. Breed clubs also hold Open shows, but these are for one breed of dog. There are also Toy Societies where dogs in the Toy Group, including Silky Terriers, are usually classified.

Championship Shows are open to any type of dog registered with the Kennel Club and over six months of age. It is by winning certain classes at Championship shows that a dog qualifies for Crufts. At Championship shows all dogs are provided with a bench space. For Toy dogs a wire cage is also provided. Dogs should be on this bench except while they are being exercised or are in the show ring. All these shows are held under Kennel Club rules.

Information about Limited, Open and Championship shows is obtained via a schedule. These give you all the details about the date of the show, the entry fee, the types of classes etc. An entry form is provided with the schedule for you to complete. To do this you will require the following information: the registered name of your dog, the date of birth, the name of the sire and dam, and the relevant class number or numbers you intend entering. If you are not sure of the classes, you should contact the breeder, who will be only too willing to help. There are also weekly canine newspapers which carry valuable information for everyone competing in dog shows.

SHOWING IN AUSTRALIA

To become a breed Champion in Australia a total of one hundred points has to be gained at four or more different shows under four or more different judges. Five points are gained for going Best of Sex, plus one point for yourself and one for every other dog beaten, over six months old of the same sex. No more than twenty-five points can be gained at any one show. Both Best Dog and Best Bitch gain points at a show in the breed. As in the UK, the youngsters have to compete with established Champions to gain their title.

There are Breed Clubs in three States, New South Wales, Western Australia and Queensland, and one in the Australian Capital Territory who hold Open shows and/or Match Events, and Championship Shows. Each State of Australia has their own Toy Group Club, plus numerous All Breed Clubs, who also hold Open Shows and/or Match Events and Championship Shows. These events are also for Trainee Judges and no Challenge points are awarded. Championship Shows are for licensed Judges where Challenge points are gained.

Ring procedure differs slightly from the UK and US once the judge has decided the placings. When the judge has indicated 1st, 2nd and 3rd, and you are lucky enough to be among them, move your dog or bitch onto placing pegs which are in the ring. If it is a small class, the judge may decide without gaiting you again, and if this is the case, move to the placing pegs once the judge has called the placings. Stand on your placing pegs until the ring steward has recorded the judge's decision on the judge's slips which are sent to the Show Office, and in some cases ribbons are handed out. You may then leave the ring.

First and second placings for each Class in each sex are required to remain at ringside for Challenge and Reserve Challenge (Championship Shows), or Best Dog/Bitch and Runner Up Best Dog/Bitch (Open Shows or Match Events). Each Class winner for the dogs will enter the ring, and the judge will then decide Challenge Dog or Best Dog, whatever the case maybe. Whatever Class this dog was entered in, the second place dog then enters the ring to compete against the other Class winners for Reserve Challenge Dog or Runner Up Best Dog. The judge will then proceed in the same manner with the bitches, judging individual Classes and then picking a Challenge Bitch (Best Bitch), and Reserve Challenge Bitch (Runner Up Best Bitch).

Now we have reached a point where we have a Best Dog and a Best Bitch, and a Reserve Dog and a Reserve Bitch. The steward will then call the Best Dog and the Best Bitch to compete against each other for Best of Breed. If the dog is Best of Breed, the Reserve Dog then enters to compete against the Best Bitch for Runner Up Best of Breed, and vice versa if the Bitch gets Best of Breed. With regard to run-offs through the different Classes of dogs and bitches, this varies in different States and Countries, and you should look into this yourself before the judging.

Now that we have a Best of Breed and a Runner Up Best of Breed, and maybe some Best Class in Breeds, it is these dogs that are required to stay for Group judging, where a Best Exhibit in Group and a Runner Up Best Exhibit in Group are decided. Once Best Exhibit in Group has been decided, the Runner Up Best of Breed for that particular breed enters the ring to compete for Runner Up Best Exhibit in Group. Best of Breed of Class will then follow for the judge to choose Best of Class in Group. All Class in Group winners are required to stay for the Best in Show judging.

7 *IN THE SHOW RING*

Y ou should bath and groom your dog the day before the show. Be aware of the distance you will have to travel to the show, and give yourself enough time so that you arrive in a stress-free state. As most shows commence judging in alphabetical order, and Australian Silkies are one of the first breeds in the ring, it is advisable to be there one hour prior to judging. This will enable you to set yourself up, pick up your catalogue and exhibit numbers if need be, and to settle your dog after the car trip. It will also help to accustom your puppy to noise, and to the presence of other dogs, before the time comes for you both to enter the show ring.

On the morning of the show you will need to take with you the dog's lead, grooming equipment, bait (special treat), water bowl and a table to groom your puppy on at the show. It is a good idea to also take water from home for the dog to drink – the puppy is used to this and will not, therefore, run the risk of being upset by other water. If you know that the show is going to be outside, you will probably need a large umbrella for shade – or for rain – and a folding chair for you to sit on.

As this is your first show, and you are a new exhibitor, you are not likely to have a carrying case, or crate, in which to transport your dog to the show. You will find one of great value, otherwise you will have to hold your dog until you are ready to go into the ring, whereas if you have a case or crate the dog could be resting until it is time for the final touch up before exhibiting. If you find that both you and your dog enjoy dog shows, there is another piece of equipment which is well worth thinking about, and that is a fold-up trolley. Avoid heavy ones; there are light aluminium ones on the market these days, and you will be the person that has to lift it in and out of your car. The trolley acts as an exercise pen and a grooming table at the show. Approximately 30 minutes prior to judging, exercise your dog, who can relieve itself and can settle down. Before you take your Silky for a walk on the grounds, be careful to check to see what other dogs are near, especially the larger breeds, as they might frighten your dog. Likewise, the Silky, being a terrier and a courageous little dog, might challenge the larger breed, which could be disastrous if the larger breed accepts the challenge.

You must try to be calm yourself, as your

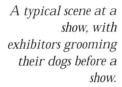

A typical scene at a show, with exhibitors grooming their dogs before a show.

nervousness will transmit itself to your dog. This being the first show for you and your dog, just remember that every exhibitor, handler and judge present once had their first show, and no one will expect your dog to perform perfectly on the first time of showing. Nor will they expect the handling to be like that of a professional. Remember, enjoy being there, and your dog will gradually get accustomed to the different surroundings and noises of a show, and in time will also enjoy being there.

PROCEDURE IN THE RING

In your show catalogue will be printed the number and name of each dog and bitch entered in the show, along with owner's name. From the catalogue you can follow the order of judging. Also, by consulting with the catalogue, you will be able to follow the judging better, as there will not always be entries in every class, and you will know how many dogs or bitches are to be judged prior to your class in which you are

entered. Each show ring has one, and frequently two, stewards – one being the ring steward who works with the judge, and the second being a gate steward who works with the exhibitors by making sure that you are at the gate entrance and ready to enter the ring once your class has been called. The breed will be called to ringside: move your dog to the ring. Take your brush with you. Allow yourself plenty of time and room to settle and groom your dog on the ground. Then your class will be called, along with your exhibit number. It is up to you to answer 'present', otherwise you stand the chance of your Silky being scratched. Your class will enter the ring and your exhibit number will be called again. If you did not answer your previous call, you have this last opportunity to do so, otherwise your Silky will be scratched, and this is final. You will have made the trip for nothing. In most countries it is a three-call system: first call for the breed, second call for class and exhibit numbers in that class, third and final call for class and exhibit numbers as the class is entering the ring

The rings are square or rectangular in shape. At times there may be different variations in ring procedure according to the judge's personal choice, but they are essentially all the same. If you are the very first dog in the ring, the ring steward will explain what the judge would like you to do. If you are first dog in your particular class, and you have not been watching what each handler before you has been doing, ask the gate steward what the judge requires. Some judges like you to go around the ring prior to tabling your Silky for conformation examination. If this is the case, the class will move around the ring together until the judge asks you to stop, and put the first dog on the table. Once the judge has completed examination and the dog has been placed on the ground, the judge will indicate that the next exhibit be placed on the table. Other judges may like you to go straight to the table, then the first dog is placed on the table for the judge's examination, and when this is completed the judge will then indicate for the next dog to be tabled.

After you have tabled your dog or bitch, and the examination for conformation has been completed, the judge will give you instructions on how you are required to 'gait' your dog. Always listen carefully at this stage, because the judge may require you to take your Silky 'straight up and back', that is move the dog away from the judge in a straight line, and then back in a straight line, bringing the dog to a stop in front of the judge. Or you might be asked to do a 'triangle', which is from a point in front of the table out to the right hand side of the ring, across the straight side of the triangle to the left side of the ring, and

then back to the point that you left from, bringing the dog to a stop in front of the judge. At this point, when you have brought your Silky back to a stop in front of the judge, it is an excellent time to tempt your exhibit with the bait (or treat). This has already been mastered in show training, as we do not want your dog jumping up – we are looking for the dog to be alert and to show well to the judge. You will then be directed where to move to, so that the judge may go through the same procedure with the other exhibits, if there are any in your class. If there are a large number of exhibits in the class, the judge may ask you to move around the ring once more together, at which time the judge will decide the placings.

At the end of your breed classes the steward will call back into the ring all the unbeaten dogs for the judge to select his Best Dog and Reserve Dog. This is repeated with the bitches. Then there is the Best Dog and Best Bitch Challenge for Best of Breed. Following this, all the unbeaten puppies are called into the ring for Best Puppy. When all the classes have finished, all the BOBs will be called into the ring to be judged for Best in Show, or, if the show is being run on the Group system, Best in Group and then Best in Show. Best Puppy in Show is judged after Best in Show.

TIPS FROM THE TOP
Three experts, who have great experience in three different aspects of showing dogs, give their views on achieving success with your Silky Terrier.

THE ART OF HANDLING
By Dayna Scales
Handling is an art. It is the technique of humans being able to work in complete

unison with their dogs. It is an ability that is acquired through experience, study and observation. There is no secret to successful handling: it can be difficult, but always try to stay calm, cool and collected. Your dog can sense your nervousness and will often take great pleasure in making the most of your vulnerable state by doing what it likes. Communicate with your dog through your tone of voice and leash control, and your Silky will respond to your commands accordingly. Be flexible with your methods of handling, depending on the personality and structure of your dog. The degree to which you succeed as a handler will be determined by your own capabilities and attitude.

Appearance and attire are also important things to consider. Dress appropriately for a Silky. For example, long flowing skirts are likely to distract your dog and could also take the judge's attention away from your dog. Colour is also an important consideration. Black pants or any dark colours are not wise behind your Silky. A bright colour or a pastel shade to show the outline of your dog is more sensible. Shoes are also very important. High heels or woollen boots do not assist when trying to demonstrate the free flowing movement of your dog. Flat, closed-in shoes, that do not have a slippery sole are suggested. No matter what you choose, always ensure that it is neat and tidy.

Showtime! Always have your dog prepared and ready to enter the show ring at least ten minutes before you are due to be judged. It is always advisable to arrive at the ringside early enough to observe the ring procedure of the judge while they are working another class or breed. Watch the patterns he or she is asking the handlers to move in. The pattern will usually remain the same throughout the rest of the classes and breeds. Always listen carefully and obey the instructions of the judge promptly. If you are a new exhibitor, and you are unsure of what to do, don't hesitate to ask for help from a fellow exhibitor, or the ring steward. They will be only too happy to assist.

There are various types of leads available from the dog shops. If possible give preference to a lightweight, easy-to-hold nylon or leather leash. Choose a colour that does not distract from your dog. Blue or black leads are good contrasting colours to an Australian Silky Terrier. Choke chains may be useful for training a dog which side-winds or crabs, or is disobedient, but they are not suggested for the show ring. If a choke chain is regularly used, the hair around the neck will break off, and, in the show ring, will always make the coat look ungroomed. Once in the ring, if there is more than one dog in your class, give yourself and other exhibitors plenty of room to move freely. Do not overcrowd other exhibitors or let your dog distract others.

A good handler is aware that you cannot use the same handling technique from one dog to another. You should adjust your speed and stacking (standing) techniques to suit the individual dog you are showing at the time. Your dogs should be trained from an early age to move with ease on either side of you. You must feel equally comfortable working the dog. Never dangle the leash from your hand; roll it up neatly in your palm so you can increase or decrease the lead length as needed. Talk to your dog while working on the lead and create a picture of smooth-flowing motion between dog and handler.

When it comes to placing your dog on the table for judging, if you are not first

Aust. Ch. Dulcannina Christabel: Each dog should be handled as an individual. This dog is stacked to show off her best points.

Aust. Ch. Dulcannina The Gremlin: Handler Michael Camac uses a different style to show this Silky, allowing the dog to be free-standing.

CS Photography.

into the ring, wait until the previous exhibit has moved away from the table. Place your dog to the front, not the middle or end of the table. This makes it easy for the judge to examine your dog. Silky Terriers should be stacked with their front legs and rear pasterns set at right angles to the table. When placing your dog into position you should use a light but firm touch. Placing one hand between your dog's hindlegs, and with the other gripping around the dog's neck, place your dog's hindquarters down first, then place the front legs, ensuring feet are turned neither in nor out. If your dog's front legs do not fall into the correct position, i.e. parallel to each other, adjust them by grasping the elbow and placing it correctly. Hind legs can be corrected by grasping the dog's hock and setting the rear pasterns perpendicular to the table.

Adjust your lead so it is placed up high on the dog's neck and settle the hair around the lead. At this stage, and only if you have time, you may wish to regroom your dog's coat. A quick and effective method of doing this is to brush the hair on the fore and hind legs up, away from the usual fall and rebrush down the legs. Then brush the body and head coat. Hold your dog's head in an erect position with the lead, gently pull the tail rearward and slightly upwards. This will make certain that the topline is straight in order to present a proper profile to the judge. You may either stand in front of the table alerting your dog, or stand behind the dog, holding the tail erect. A slight prompting from behind the ears may encourage your dog to prick its ears.

As the judge approaches the table and if your dog looks to back off away from the judge, gently pull the dog's tail backwards towards the end of the table. This will encourage the dog to lean forward, against your pressure, and therefore to stand up correctly. Similarly, if your dog will not allow the judge to examine the hindquarters, pull the dog's head towards the front of the table and your dog should stand. This procedure can also be done when training puppies for table examination. Another training hint is to set your dog up on your legs and slowly move your legs. This will allow your dog to feel at ease on an unstable table.

When the judge is going over your dog, do not be distracted, but keep your dog under control at all times. Be aware of your dog's legs moving out of the correct position. Do not fiddle; only move a leg when needed and do it without fuss. Always take notice of what the judge is doing. If, after examination, the judge wishes to have another general overview of your Silky, ensure your dog looks at his or her best, and reset the dog if necessary. After the judge has assessed your dog, do not spend a lot of time brushing the dog or fiddling with the lead. Your lead should be set in position, high up on the neck; you can do this while the judge is going over the rear end of your dog.

As a judge, I usually request a triangle pattern. This allows me to assess the fore and hindquarter movement and observe the dog in profile, evaluating drive, reach and topline carriage. Your responsibility as a handler is to make sure your dog moves in straight lines away from, and back to, the judge. Focus on an object and head towards it, and then go straight back to the judge, while, of course, checking your dog's movement. Take notice of the area available to you. Plan how far you are going to go in order for the judge to see your dog's movement clearly. Moving with your dog should be natural and easy. You cannot project this picture with your dog held up on a tight lead. Any time a correction is necessary while in motion, it should be done quietly and with as little opposing motion to your line of travel as possible. Talk to your dog constantly, encouraging your dog to be animated. Upon returning to the judge, stop at least a metre in front of the judge. You will want to free-stand your Silky. The easiest way to do this is to animate your dog by baiting. Unfortunately, some dogs will bait and some will not. Bait is anything that will attract and lure your dog. Food such as baked beef liver, or heart in particular, is most commonly used, although small toys or favourite objects may be effective. Work the bait according to your dog's responses. If the dog needs more encouragement, offer only small pieces at a time, to keep the dog's attention and interest in you. Through the usage of bait and the lead, you may be able to set your dog up without 'man-handling'. If you feel your dog's legs are not placed correctly, by slightly pulling the lead to your right, your dog will place the right foot forward, without moving the hindlegs. If you pull the lead to your left, the dog will reposition the left leg forward. Of course this will only happen with training at home, and at dog shows. A good way of perfecting setting up your Silky on the table and on the ground, is to watch yourself in the mirror. Try various methods of stacking, maybe getting someone else to show your dog for you, so you can observe.

When you are in a line-up or waiting, you should take the view that you are only in the show ring for a short time, and so show your dog at all times. You can never be sure when the judge is going to glance over and

It's never too young to learn the art of handling. Rebecca Hingeley is pictured with Tarawera Cats winning the 7 to under 12 years Pal Jnr Showman for Western Australia.

make comparisons. By saying this, I do not mean you should tire or bore your dog by constantly standing it up. Relax your dog by talking, and playing etc. – while watching the judge's action, and ensuring your dog's legs are not positioned in a detrimental way when the judge may glance in your direction. Silkies should appear to be showing themselves. Allow your dog to be alert and look at the surroundings. For final presentation to the judge, do not expect your Silky to stand like a statue – after all, they are Terriers. Do not harshly correct puppies that are misbehaving, let them have fun, otherwise boredom may soon set in.

Never mimic another handler. Know your dog's shortcomings as well as good qualities. This way, you will be able to create a clear visual impression of your own dog that you wish to convey to the judge. With successful preparation, you will never encounter any situation inside or outside the ring that you will not be able to handle. Be a good sport, accept your placing graciously. Remember, your aim on entering a show is to get a judge's opinion of your dog. Accept it as such, always allowing the judge the same respect for their opinion as you would demand for your own. Through your actions, you are creating reactions and leaving impressions good or bad. At each show you are exhibiting not only for the judge inside the ring, but also for spectators outside the ring. If you are in desperate need of throwing a tantrum, wait until you are well away from the ring and other exhibitors. Make sure your conduct is that of a true sportsman and remember to praise your dog for a job well done. No matter how experienced or inexperienced you are, you can always learn and improve on ways to show off your dogs to their best advantage. Watch other exhibitors and experienced handlers, or watch the junior handlers competition. Some of these young people have handling dogs down to a fine art. To be a good handler means that you can show a dog at any time in any situation, always making a good impression on the judge and other exhibitors. Remember that we are out there because of our love for the breed, and we do enjoy showing them off. There can be no more beautiful sight to behold than a freshly bathed, well-groomed and coated Silky Terrier, in full flight around the show ring.

WHAT THE JUDGE IS LOOKING FOR
P.J. Hingeley: Western Australia

As a breeder and Toy judge, I would like to elaborate more on the characteristics and general appearance of the breed in relation to what judges are looking for, and which make the Australian Silky Terrier different from other breeds. Type is very important, after all it is type which sets each breed apart from each other. We can have a very sound cross-bred dog or bitch with no particular type, and if that dog entered the show ring as an Australian Silky Terrier I would not consider it because the dog does not resemble one, i.e. Type. That is not to say that judges will ignore soundness, but one likes to hope that they will find a sound dog or bitch with a correctness of type. When considering correctness of type for this breed, it is well to keep in mind that the present-day Australian Silky is not a long-coated Australian Terrier, neither is it a poor-type Yorkshire Terrier, or one of the many in between impostors of the recent past.

Dogs presented for appraisal should be in such a condition that they will appeal in like fashion as demanded in the Standard under 'General Appearance'. Each part should appear in all respects balanced to other parts, making up the whole animal. It is important that proper size, shape and substance be recognised, having in mind the weight 3.6 to 4.5 kgs. (8 to 10 lbs.) and height of approximately 23 cms (9 inches) at shoulder point, bitches slightly less, and a well ribbed up body, with emphasis on refinement in bone and build throughout. The Australian Silky is not a square dog like the Yorkshire, nor rather long in proportion to height as in the Australian Terrier, but of medium length.

Characteristics in any breed are of paramount importance, as these are salient to that particular breed, and being a

*Aust. Ch.
Dulcannina
Cheyene being
assessed by British
judge Tom Horner.*

*Photo:
K. Barkleigh-Shute.*

Terrier, the Australian Silky in the show ring must display very keen alertness, and should be sound and actively interested in surrounding proceedings. It is therefore very hard to keep an Australian Silky still for a great length of time, as they should always be either moving their head and ears, or turning about looking for something that will attract them. It is also a characteristic of the breed to occasionally raise one foot when standing. They should not be penalised for any of these characteristics.

The head is required to be strong, showing Terrier character. The balance of foreface to forehead is most important. The ears must always be small and 'V' shaped, and carried high on the head. The neck is important in balance, a refined neck is required with sufficient length to have a slight crest. Movement must be smooth and elastic, the fore-end action straight from the shoulder and directly associated with strength and drive from the hindquarters, stifle and hock. No allowance may be made at either end for faulty construction. Feet are another important feature, being small and cat-like with toes close knit; large or flat feet are not characteristic.

The coat must be fine, glossy and silky textured and straight, and a length of 13 to 15 cms (5 to 6 inches) body coat is desirable for major awards, but must not impede the dog's action in any way. The coat is to be measured at the withers, and, with the correct length of coat, you will be able to see the dog's feet and a certain amount of daylight under them. Naturally coat grows from under the stomach, but do not let anyone convince you that this should be 13 to 15 cms. Colour is clearly defined in the Standard allowing only for Blue and Tan, or Grey-Blue and Tan, the richer of these colours the better. Blue is the prime word here, and Grey-Blue does not mean nearly White.

After examining and assessing the virtues of each dog in a class, it is then for the individual Judge to interpret the Standard to the best of their ability, and it may not always be the best coloured exhibit that

The Silky head should be strong, showing distinctive Terrier character.

Coat and colour are important points to assess.

wins but a better mover displaying more Terrier expression or alertness. There are breeders who claim faults in their own dogs as virtues, and judges who do not know the difference are doing incalculable harm to the Australian Silky Terrier. Judges should look for Australian Silky Terriers that show life and vitality in sound, free action; that stand in the centre of the ring, head up, ears and tail erect; that look the judge in the eye and '*ask for it*'.

JUDGING SILKY TERRIERS

By D. White, all-breeds international judge.
It is well over 30 years since I first had the pleasure of judging the Australian Silky Terrier. Being an all-breed judge, I feel that all-breeders give an all-round judgement, as distinct from the specialists, who mostly fault judge. The all-breeder judges for the best point and has learned from the start not to fault judge. OK, you say, but what happens when you have two great specimens in front of you, and you have to

When judging, first impressions are usually the best.

make a final decision! You still can find the better point on one than the other.

Getting back to our Silky, first impressions are usually best. Look for the general appearance of the dogs in the class. Naturally the dogs and bitches must show the Terrier characteristics, alertness, be active and be sound. The movement should be free and tight at the elbows. The front legs should move straight when coming toward you, and should move neither too close nor too wide from behind. Colour is a difficult consideration, because judges have room for much variation in their decisions: "Blue and tan or grey-blue and tan, the richer the better. Blue on the tail should be very dark." Unfortunately some judges have a tendency to award dogs with very light colours, both tan and blue. Black colour is allowed in puppies up until the age of 18 months.

Mouths should be watched and a scissor bite is essential. Ears should be V-shaped with a fine leather, pricked and free from hair. Dark eyes, the darker the better. A nice level topline, the body slightly longer than the height of the dog. A flat coat, glossy and of a silky texture, about 13 to 15 cms. long, from behind the ears to the set on of tail, but remember the coat must not impede the movement of the dog. There are many other things to remember when judging Silkies, but the main thing to picture in your mind, is the General Appearance, Movement, Coat and Colour of Coat, Bite and Temperament.

8 BREEDING SILKY TERRIERS

If you wondering about breeding from your Silky, you must consider your reasons for taking this step. Are you going to keep a puppy for a pet, or do you think mating will mature your bitch? These do not constitute vaid reasons for putting your bitch through all the upheaval of having a litter. Equally, some people are of the opinion that all bitches should have at least one litter, yet they cannot give a reasonable explanation about why they think this. Are you hoping to show, or you may already be into showing? Perhaps you want to produce a youngster for the show ring for yourself that is of a higher quality than both parents. You must have an objective in mind. Ideally you should aim to obtain a better dog or bitch, while, at the same time, improving the breed. Silkies can have litters of three to four pups or more, and they should all be as sound, both physically and mentally, as you can produce. If your bitch's lines are noted for problems, do not breed any more of that particular line, otherwise this will only give us, the breeders, a bad name, and you will do yourself and the breed a disservice in mating your bitch. Have your vet check the bitch for problems such as severe hip dysplasia. The same applies to the dog that you choose for the mating. He should be sound in body and temperament and be free of major genetic problems. Remember, although no dog is perfect, you should only use dogs and bitches of the highest quality.

You must also consider the cost and time involved in breeding. There is the stud fee – that is the fee for using your chosen dog; this fee should be paid at the time of mating. Any animals being used for breeding must be in first class-condition, be up-to-date with all injections, and be fully wormed. All the puppies will require regular feeding, worming, inoculations and lots of human attention. There will be a lot of money going out before you receive a penny for the sale of a puppy.

BREEDING PROGRAMMES

RANDOM MATING
This is the type of mating such as occurs in a pack of wild dogs. It is not a breeding system, but something which, unfortunately, takes place in the backyards of irresponsible breeders. Regrettably, the progeny often supply a high percentage of the pet market and pet shops, and often

their pedigrees and registrations are of dubious nature.

MATING LIKE TO LIKE

This is a system based on the theory that 'like begets like'. It is a wasteful mating because like does not always beget like. The probability of getting what you want is low, and even if you are fortunate enough to produce it, the chances of the type, in turn, being able to reproduce itself (of being 'prepotent') is low.

INBREEDING

This is the mating of closely related individuals. There is nothing inherently bad or wrong with inbreeding, despite the widely accepted and traditional attitudes on this practice. Criticism of the practice, or its results, stems from breeders using unsuitable stock in the first place. Neither is there anything inherently good about it. The use of inbreeding to its advantage requires a comprehensive knowledge of the basic hereditary principles of pedigrees, and of the ancestors and their faults and attributes. It is a system designed to duplicate the good points and concentrate them in progeny, i.e. to increase 'homozygosity' for as many desirable characters as possible. It is a practice which, to be successful, requires the mating of individuals as closely related as possible, e.g. parent/child, brother/sister etc. The advantages are that it fixes type more quickly; it results in less variation in type in a litter; it is a good test of the bloodline; it fixes desirable characteristics in the homozygous state, which renders the individual more prepotent. The disadvantages are that the practice affects all genes. Faults and undesirable characteristics are fixed, as well as the good points. It

really requires absolutely outstanding individuals, which are rare. Breeders tend to be a little kennel-blind and often have inflated opinions of their stock, and sometimes severe culling of the resultant litter is necessary – a difficult practice for a dog-lover to come to terms with.

LINEBREEDING

This is the most common and popular method among breeders. It is based on the mating together of individuals, within a particular line of descent to an ancestor of outstanding merit. For linebreeding to be successful it must be continued, and also the individual that one is linebreeding to must be familiar – the dog's type, temperament, faults and attributes. It is no use linebreeding to an unknown fantasy. Linebreeding to an individual more than two or three generations back is, effectively, a waste of time, compared to inbreeding at the level of the third generation. An individual needs to appear on the pedigree four times to have as much genetic influence on the pups as the sire or dam. Most breeders are great believers in linebreeding, but in Silkies the time comes when the line is too inbred; then an outcrossing should be done to bring strength back into the line and, maybe, a more outgoing nature.

OUT CROSSING

is when two unrelated dogs are mated. It is used by breeders to attempt to introduce characters or attributes not present in their own line. This method will not help the breeder to establish 'type'. It should only be used occasionally, returning back to the linebreeding pattern later. It must be remembered that, apart from the good points, there will be some bad. One must be very careful: good points can be improved on slowly, bad points are hard to remove.

CROSSBREEDING

This is not allowed by Kennel Controls today. But not long ago it was an allowed practice – for example, the use of an Australian Silky Terrier with a Yorkshire Terrier.

THE BROOD BITCH

Everyone must start somewhere and breeders start with a foundation bitch. A bitch for breeding should be a little rugged, of medium size, not too fat or lean, with a well curved rib cage, a calm bitch with a good disposition, a certain amount of aggression and a sensible bitch with a will of her own. This type of bitch always seems to have a good whelping record. Bitches that have been spoilt may not be good brood bitches even though structurally super – this is the kind of bitch that declines even to assist her own labour pains. However, this may not always be the case. If ever there is one department where the best laid plans can go wrong, it is in whelping.

So much can be done to aid your breeding. First, select a healthy bitch. The most important thing should be soundness – a bitch with a nice head, good dark eyes, well-placed ears, a level topline, a good front, small catlike feet, a good mouth, good hindquarters, a nice textured coat of dark blue with a rich tan, tail carried just right, combined with great temperament and movement. Your breeding bitch must be the best you have, *not the one that's no good to show but OK for breeding*. Is this a bitch fit to be bred from – pedigree, type, conformation and temperament? It is hard to get objective assessment on a dog, hard to be objective about your own dog. Consider the opinion of her breeder; the opinion of other breeders or breed enthusiasts; and the opinion of judges, and her show performance. However, the final decision rests with you. Look at her pedigree; her faults; her attributes.

By now your bitch has had her first season, at about seven to nine months of age. The actual age is not of vital importance, unless she is either too young or too old. Really no bitch should be mated under fifteen months – the onset of her first or second season is not the onset of maturity. Although nature originally intended it to be possible to have a litter at this age, it is not proper. The bitch is not fully mature, she is much too young to possess the calm that only maturity brings. Also, do not wait until your bitch is four or five years old before she has the first litter. Have your bitch checked before mating, check her health and weight – overweight bitches are very lazy whelpers. To check her weight just run your hand over the rib cage, which should have a layer of fat, not rolls of fat.

WHEN TO MATE

A bitch comes into season twice a year, although there are those who do not have their first season until they are 12 to 14 months old, and then only once a year. The season is detected by a coloured discharge which can be from a very heavy bleeding to a very faint colour. Most Silkies keep themselves spotless, so in some cases the first few days can go undetected. If you plan to mate on this season, it might be necessary to swab her twice a day. You might also consider having a smear taken by a vet, to detect when the bitch is

ABOVE: Aust. Ch. Ensta
Fancy Freeby: Highly
successful in the show ring
and as a brood bitch.

Photo: Cabal.

RIGHT: Aust. Ch.
Dulcannina To The Max:
A son of Aust. Ch. Ensta
Fancy Freeby.

ovulating. You should inform the stud dog's owner about the likely day for the mating.It is not uncommon for the young bitch to go very quiet and withdrawn during her season. However, others will flirt with other dogs, or even the cat, by turning their rear end to them and turning their tail to one side. Some bitches have what is called a 'blind' or 'quiet' season; this is when they show very little colour, if any. Another sign of the bitch in season is the swelling of the vulva and the area around it. The bitch may also be seen to leave her mark in the garden, similar to a cat marking its territory. It is important to mark the first day of the bitch's season on your calendar. During the second stage of the season, the discharge will fade and the vulva will continue to swell, and will become very soft and receptive. If you touch the lower part of the bitch's spine, she will switch her tail right round, displaying her condition. She is now ready for mating. This is usually from the twelfth to the fourteenth day. Unfortunately not all bitches are the same, some can be mated on the fourth day of colour and take, yet others will not entertain a dog until much later. Unfortunately there is no set rule regarding ovulation.

THE MATING

The first mating act lasts, in general, from ten to fifteen minutes; sometimes some subjects prolong it unreasonably, up to forty minutes. Do not become upset at this; try not to frighten them, talk to your bitch, pat her head, aid her to free herself without a shock; remember this is all new to her. Two matings, twenty-four or forty-eight hours apart, are sufficient, and give you, the breeder, a better chance of covering the ovulation period. If you need to travel a

great distance to the stud dog, stay over if possible. Some bitches will become stressed in strange surroundings, and this could delay ovulation for a day or two.

When a stud is intelligent and experienced, and the bitch is ready, willing and responsive, the two can be left together (but observed) for nature to take her course. Let them flirt and play; this stimulates them both into an easy and happy mating. This way there is minimum interference. Some assistance may be required. When the stud dog mounts the bitch, hold her hindquarters; this will stop her from sitting down. The dog may need a little leverage to get closer to the bitch. If he is too far away, he can end up going over or under and each side of the target. If this occurs, gently move the bitch backwards as he starts to work. As he finds the vulva he will move forward and up, treading as he tries to gain a better tie with the bitch. Once this is done, the dog will attempt to get off the bitch to the side – to turn. Hold the two sets of hindquarters together until the glands of the penis fully dilate and tie the two dogs together. It is a good idea to hold both dogs together just in case the dog slips out. Once the tie is made, hold the bitch. She may object strenuously as the glands of the penis swell to form the tie. Hold her very firmly: she will soon settle down and will accept the fact she can do nothing about it. Always keep the bitch's rear up off the ground when the mating is over. Attend to the bitch, put her away and attend to the dog. Make sure his penis has gone back into the sheath and all the hair is out, wash him with warm water, and let them both rest.

THE STUD DOG

Selection of a sire is very important because

of the many choices available, and because it is more complicated. Considerations are, firstly, the same as those for the bitch, i.e. pedigree, type, conformation and temperament. But further considerations are necessary and they relate to the dog's suitability to the bitch. The dog and bitch must complement each other in all of the above-mentioned criteria. A successful stud dog can have a tremendous genetic influence on a breed in a very short period of time. A popular, widely used stud can flood the breed with his genetics within a couple of years. He will do this with his good points and bad points simultaneously.

Do not wait until the last minute to choose the stud dog – the dog should have something positive to offer your bitch before you consider him as a mate. Do not be afraid to discuss the positives and negatives with the stud dog's owner; most owners are only too willing to exchange ideas and help in any way they can. Look at what the dog is producing, assess his progeny. Look at the suitability of the dog's type for your bitch, and whether it will correct any major problem in your bitch. For a maiden bitch use an older dog with experience, and one that has already got progeny in the show ring. Consider his bloodline with your bitch's pedigree (remember do not go too close). The more he resembles his genetic bloodlines, the more he is likely to reproduce his type. A dog which is prepotent for good body type will generally become a strong foundation dog in a pedigree. A dog like this can often be inbred upon, when further back in a pedigree. One should not assess a stud dog until his oldest progeny are about eighteen months; by this time his off-spring will have shaped up. Cheap stud dogs with no strings attached often fall into one of the following

Aust. Ch. Bowenvale Sir Rex: One of the greatest foundation dogs for the breed in Australia and overseas.

areas. One is that he has never been shown. Or the stud dog owner may try to persuade you by saying "Look at the Champions on his pedigree" – but this does not mean that the dog himself is a good specimen. The owner may make excuses, such as saying they themselves have not been well and that has restricted the dog's show career. Or the owner may say "He is very sound, just look at him." The cheapest stud dog may be in your own backyard, but unless he is a good example of the breed and complements your bitch's bloodlines, *don't*. Think before you mate. Some stud dogs may be free because a breeder may have a young dog they wish to break in; or the breeder may want your bitch to go to their dog if your bitch is a good specimen of the breed or has very good bloodlines. In most cases like that the stud dog breeder will always want the pick of the litter. You may also be offered a free mating, but on condition that the owner of the stud will take two puppies to sell to recoup the stud fee. But remember – your bitch may only have two puppies!

You have already discussed bloodlines and show history with the stud dog's owner. The polite method is to notify the owner of the stud dog you would like to use over your bitch. Just like you, the dog's owner prefers to have bitches of good calibre and suitable bloodlines to be mated to their dog. Once all is agreed, that the bitch can go to the dog, and the stud fee is settled, you need only to wait for your bitch to come into season, and when the time arrives, ring the stud dog's owner giving the approximate date of mating. This allows the owner to plan around other bitches that may be coming in for a mating.

The stud dog's owner will give you a copy of the dog's pedigree and relevant certificates, and a stud receipt. This reminds you of the exact date of mating and is useful for the bitch's owner when filling out the puppies' registrations forms. The owner of the stud dog should not give the owner of the bitch a Service Certificate until after the second mating has taken place and the stud fee is paid in full. If the bitch misses, the situation regarding the stud fee which has been paid is that, in most cases, the stud owner will be willing for the bitch to come back on her next season. Or the stud dog owner may give you half the stud fee back if you, as owner of the bitch, do not want a return mating.

ARTIFICIAL INSEMINATION

In many areas around the world artifical insemination is now common practice. It can be done by your vet, or, possibly, a very experienced breeder. Artificial insemination could be the way forward: it places no strain on the dog or bitch, and saves time. For some bitches that cannot be mated naturally, and for elderly dogs, artificial insemination may be the only method. To collect the semen from the dog and transfer it into the bitch is not difficult; all that is needed is a sterile jar and a length of tubing. All this must be sterile and dry, just a drop of water or blood will destroy the sperm. One main point to remember about semen collection is that the semen must at all times remain warm and be kept away from light.

CARE OF THE IN-WHELP BITCH

Three weeks after the mating your bitch should be wormed to promote her health and to enable her to derive all possible benefit from her food. This must not be done any later than three weeks, as it could harm the litter. The gestation period is the time from mating to whelping; on average this is 63 days, or nine weeks. Silkies are good time-keepers, usually whelping on time. The expectant mother should be treated as normal during the first few weeks. It is not until the fifth or sixth week that you will be sure she has taken and is in whelp. There are days when you can decide your bitch has taken, only to be unsure a few days later. Some seem to carry their puppies high up to the ribcage, while others carry them low. It is not until the last ten days, when the puppies have "dropped" that you can be sure. Again, each bitch is different. You will soon learn to read your girls. It is possible to have your bitch scanned to see if she is in whelp or not. This can be done between day 28 and day 30.

It is not until about the sixth week, maybe a little earlier if she is carrying a large litter, that there should be a change in the diet. Give her small meals throughout the day, to ease the discomfort felt by one large meal. Feed only top-quality foods. There are a considerable number of firms producing feeds for bitches in whelp, these contain all the necessary extras required during gestation. However, if you are feeding meat, the ration may be doubled during the first month of gestation. Towards the end of gestation add to each meal a quarter teaspoon of calcium glauconite. Do not give too much calcium under the pretext that you wish to ensure solid bone in the pups. An excess of calcium can cause a soldering of bones of the foetus. Also, twice a week, you may give her about 13.05 grams Vitamin C, increase her vegetables and offer a nice large veal bone to gnaw. (Some people always give their bitches in whelp, from ten days after mating to ten days before whelping, one Raspberry Leaf tablet.)

Remember the bitch gives of her very self, drawing upon her own vitality in order that a new generation can be born. She must be strong and healthy, and have a good supply of nourishment, minerals and vitamins if she is to bring a good healthy litter into our world. Foods that contain calcium include tomatoes, beans, meat, carrots, eggs, milk, cheese, buttermilk, oranges and spinach. Iron is found in liver, spinach, heart, eggs, fish, whole-wheat bread, onions, bananas, beans and milk.

Always seek the vet's advice if you feel anything is amiss at any time. If something has gone wrong, the sooner the vet treats the bitch, the better chance she has of delivering live puppies. As she becomes heavy, prevent her from jumping up – a difficult thing to do with Silkies. Normal exercise should be taken, as should bathing and daily grooming, making sure her claws are kept short to prevent any possible damage to the new-born puppies.

9 *WHELPING AND REARING*

Make preparations for the whelping in advance. Do not be caught unawares. You will need a box of a comfortable size for your bitch. An oblong one is much more suitable than a round one, and it also does not want to be too large, otherwise she will lose the pups in it. Avoid baskets, as these harbour insects and mites. Cut part of the front out, which can be put back in place when the puppies are beginning to move around. Line this with a good thickness of newspaper. However, if you plan to have further litters, provided this one runs smoothly, you might find it better to invest in a purpose-built whelping box. The good ones are made from a non-absorbent material and are enclosed, with a hinged lid and double front-doors. They are usually fully insulated, so extra heat may not be necessary if the room being used is heated. They also dismantle easily, without the need for tools. They are tall enough to prevent the bitch from trying to climb out and large enough for her to stretch out full length either way. However, some breeders consider it better to whelp your bitch in a cardboard box and then, after she has whelped, put her and the puppies into your nice whelping box. A heat pad is useful to help dry the whelps soon after birth, especially if they are arriving quickly. Puppies will settle well on these warm pads, particularly if they are covered with old flannelette sheets. Thus the mother is able to have a slight rest between tending to one new arrival and awaiting the birth of the next. If you are using an open-topped whelping box, then an infra-red lamp can be used, making sure that the heat is gentle over the delicate puppies. It is very important to make sure that all electrical equipment is safe; check it carefully before it is required. Some books recommend having a small shoe-box with a hot water bottle and blanket available in which to put the whelps while another is on the way. However, some people have followed these instructions, only to find that this distresses the mother too much. If this is the case, use the hot water bottle wrapped in a blanket within the whelping box, moving it around, depending on where the mother is. This way she does not become distressed, because she can see and smell her puppies. Also it means you are handling them as little as possible, otherwise the mother can become distressed until she is confident about what you are doing. You will also need any amount of clean old towels or sheets, which can be destroyed after use, and a good supply of clean newspaper. You may also need to have in readiness some strong thread, in case you need to tie the umbilical cord, and a pair of sterilised rounded-end scissors for cutting it. You will also need a pair of scales to weigh each pup and a notebook, pen and clock for jotting down the series of events as they happen – i.e. the time the bitch seriously started to bed-make, the time of the last feed, the time of straining, the times of the births, etc. All these details will be very helpful for your vet, should you need to call for assistance. Lastly, the vet's telephone number should be easily available, just in case. Even though the majority of confinements are without complication, it is advisable, as soon as there are any indications of complications, to ring your vet. In spite of all your goodwill, the vet alone may eventually be the only one able to save the bitch and her litter by the use of forceps, or by caesarean operation.

Do not let your bitch decide where she wants to whelp – she will prefer somewhere under a bed. With a maiden bitch let her sleep in the whelping box occasionally. It is not until a few days prior to the whelping date that you should make her use it instead of her normal bed. As the day draws nearer, make sure she has plenty of paper and bedding in the box to scratch about in and make her bed. This she will do time after time, so be patient. So you decide on the place, then keep her quiet and well away from other dogs and people. Your bedroom is a good place in which to put the whelping box; then you can keep an eye on her at night without having to keep getting up.

EARLY STAGES OF LABOUR

Although Silkies tend to be punctual, be prepared for the bitch to whelp anything from three days before to three days after the due date. Puppies can arrive and be perfectly normal anything between six days early or four days late but keep a close watch on your bitch. The first signs of whelping are a drop in temperature and the bitch will refuse to eat. Do not force her – it is quite useless having indigestion complicating her task. Most bitches do not eat when the time arrives, though some will eat right up until the last moment. She will become very restless and do a great deal of digging and scratching of her box. If she wants to go out to relieve herself, let her do so, but go with her, armed with a torch if this happens at night-time, just in case she whelps outside. This stage can continue for a great length of time, anything from one hour to twenty-four hours. If the bitch is very spoiled – aren't they all? – you can help her by speaking gently, repeating her name and assuring her that you are near. Most bitches at this time have a real need for the presence of their masters. Then she may start panting, and may not want to move. These are all signs that her time is near. A water sack may be the first thing you actually see, and this can remain in place for some time. It looks dark, is round and spongy, and its purpose is to lubricate the birth canal.

THE WHELPING

Once the bitch starts straining at regular intervals and the water sack is expelled, she should produce the first puppy within the hour. She will start pushing, either in a squatting position, or lying down. As she does this, you will notice that her tail stands straight up. She will rest and then start

ABOVE: *Silky puppies aged three days. Note their tails have been docked.*

LEFT: *A bitch puppy, pictured at two days old. This pup, Marshdae Mamunna, became an important brood bitch.*

again. Remember, particularly if this is her first litter, to remain close, massaging her back gently from the head toward the tail. Never massage the stomach, it may cause serious complications. A bitch experiencing her first confinement is nearly always panic-stricken by what is happening to her, and sometimes she will forget all that she should know by instinct. Puppies are usually born head first, the puppy arriving within the amniotic sac. This should be opened as soon as possible by the bitch using her teeth. She will then lick the whelp, clearing the mucus and fluid from the nose and mouth. By this time you will have see the puppy move about and heard the puppy cry. The bitch should then move to the umbilical cord, which she should bite clear. But sometimes with maiden bitches, when the first puppy arrives, they just look at it in astonishment. Then you must help the puppy to get rid of the amniotic sack.

The afterbirth follows the puppy. This may be still attached, or the umbilical cord often breaks several inches from the puppy's stomach. Force the mother to sniff the puppy while you gently remove the gelatinous membrane to free the pup. Pinch the cord firmly with your forefinger and thumb of the left hand, snip the cord with clean scissors about one-and-a-half to two inches from the body, and give the pup a good rub with a clean dry towel to ensure the pup does not get cold. Then place the puppy in the whelping box with the bitch, who will then proceed to lick the puppy well. Although, as has been said, some bitches will bite the umbilical cord themselves, some breeders like to cut the umbilical cord to make sure the break is far enough away from the puppy's stomach. Some breeders allow the bitch to eat the foetal envelope on the grounds that it contains substances necessary for her health. However, others strongly maintain that this just makes the bitch sick and that she is only cleaning up. Those breeders remove the foetal envelopes as they appear, and keep a careful count. Sometimes the bitch is too busy with the arrival of the next whelp to care for the preceding one. Then you will have to break open the sack and, if you cannot get the mother to wash the puppy's face to clear the airways, use a very soft warm towel to dab the nose and mouth, encourage the mouth open, and hold the whelp's head down to help drain the fluid away. You should then feel the puppy wriggling about.

The afterbirths may follow each puppy but occasionally there can be several puppies born in a rush, and then the afterbirths may follow in a little group. Do not panic, just remember each pup has an afterbirth, so keep count when the bitch has finished whelping. The numbers should tally. If the puppies are born without them, do not hesitate for a second – call the vet: it is extremely dangerous for the mother to retain the afterbirths, and she will run the risk of infection.

With the first puppy warm and dry you now await the second pup which could take up to one hour. Most bitches produce pups without too much help, some hardly seem to contract, the puppies just pop out like peas from a pod. You can also help your bitch if a pup, beginning to arrive, gets stuck and, despite all the straining and groaning, will not move. Take a clean dry towel and *very very* delicately help the pup to free itself. You must not pull, for this could tear the mother, you must follow the efforts of the bitch. Gently pull out and down, at a 45 degrees angle. If the puppy is presenting head first, put your first two fingers on either side of the neck just behind the head, pull gently and curl your

fingers back into your hand as you pull. If the puppy is coming feet first, pull gently above the hocks. The head and shoulders will be caught very firmly inside the bitch. Gently put your little finger up the side and hook out one elbow, repeat from the other side. Then pull the puppy out and down. Once the shoulders are through, the puppy will pop out very easily. Never grab the puppy around the stomach, you can rupture the puppy's liver. Only pull when the bitch is bearing down.

Do not worry about the bitch stepping on her puppies: this does not seem to happen. However, while she is giving birth to the remaining litter, this is where the box containing the hot water bottle comes in handy, as a place in which to put the puppies and keep them warm and prevent them becoming wet again from the latest arrival. On an average, puppies arrive 30 to 45 minutes apart. The bitch will rest during these pauses and will encourage the puppies to take nourishment from her milk bar. As each puppy arrives, record the weight, sex and time of arrival. An average weight is four to five ounces; any less than this must be watched carefully. If it is a large litter, the little one could be pushed away, so you might have to supplement the food. Your vet would advise on this. There are tiny bottles for feeding and special powdered milk – do not try feeding anything else. When you feel she has finished whelping, offer her a drink. she will then settle down to her brood, having gathered them close to her, and sleep. When all this is done, look at your bitch. With her progeny between her flanks she is prodigiously happy – and so are you.

POST-WHELPING CARE
Silky Terriers are relatively good whelpers

as a rule. Strangely enough, it cannot be said that a small bitch is no good for breeding nor that a larger one is better. This has been disproved many times. Actually many brood bitches are larger to comply more fully with the Standard regarding weight and size, but many a top dog has been bred from a small bitch – though not a very tiny one. The average size of Silky litters is three to four; this is a nice litter for a bitch to rear. However, larger litters do occur, as many as six or eight pups is not uncommon. With this size litter your bitch may need help, and you could supplement the pups' early-morning and late-at-night meals. For slow puppies, that do not suck the bitch, give them one drop of brandy, with drops of calcium sandoz or honey, mixed with warm water. Make up 2 mls. You can also add one drop of gripe water. Alternatively use a multi-vitamin solution, which is much more accurate and faster acting. Have it ready before the bitch whelps (it may be needed).

For some reason we think that an animal should have no difficulty in having her pups. This is not true; just like humans, things can go wrong. We now have the Caesarean; this can be a great comfort for you the breeder, but a Caesarean, if possible, should be your last choice. Remember a human who has a Caesarean is kept off her feet for about ten days, or as long as necessary, but not your bitch. From the time she comes out of the anaesthetic she feeds her pups and attends to maternal duties before being physically able to do so. She has more strength than good sense.

Some bitches, especially with a first litter, are not interested in their puppies until they have finished whelping and have rested. If your bitch is one of these, then place the puppies on a heating pad or a warm hot water bottle under a blanket. Young pups are like babies and need to be kept warm; if this is not done, they will cry continuously. When the bitch has rested she will settle down and want her puppies. Give her a clean bed of newspaper and vet bed and a warm drink, made up of two cups of milk, and the yolk of one egg. Give one tablespoon of milk of magnesia, which will help clean the bitch out, three to four times a day. No solid food for two to three hours.

Newspaper is warm for the whelping box and easily disposed of. Never put small pieces of blankets in the whelping box with very young puppies, as the bitch, for sure, will dig it up and bury her puppies in the blanket, and may suffocate them. If you are a novice breeder, it is a good idea to have your vet check your bitch when whelping is over to make sure all is well. Sometimes they retain an afterbirth from one pup, but just one injection will soon produce it. If you cannot get to a vet, then the tablespoon of milk of magnesia can help. After two days, if you wish, your bitch may need a wash. Clean her with a cloth soaked in a weak but tepid solution of bicarbonate of soda. Keep her bedding clean at all times.

ECLAMPSIA

Watch for any sign of milk fever (eclampsia) in your bitch. Milk fever is the result of calcium being drained from the body to a degree that causes the bitch to collapse. Usually, if this is going to happen, it occurs within the first three weeks. It has been known for a bitch come down with eclampsia at eight days. The first signs are that the bitch will refuse food. She will look starry-eyed and have a rapid respiration rate. Occasionally she may show signs of lameness. She will not feed the pups and she will have a high temperature. If this goes unnoticed, she will then develop generalised muscle-twitching and shaking, will often be unable to walk or stand and have a very rapid respiration rate. Handle her very gently and talk to her quietly. Noises and bright lights could set off convulsions. Do not delay. She will need immediate attention by a vet: it is a matter of life and death – intravenous calcium as soon as possible is her only hope. This is given very slowly; if given too fast it will slow the heart down too rapidly. When a bitch has milk fever, the heart is beating very rapidly. The vet monitors the heart rate as the calcium is given, and the amount that is needed by the bitch varies. Once the heart rate settles down to normal, or if beat irregularities are appearing, the calcium must be stopped. As the blood calcium levels improve so the muscle spasm, twitching and respiration rate becomes almost normal. Your bitch that was near dying a few minutes earlier will stand up, not knowing what all the fuss is about. It is not necessary to remove the puppies away from the dam. If she has been given intravenous calcium and she is now steady, there should not be a re-occurrence. It could harm the puppies' digestion if they were taken away from the bitch and fed substitute milk.

CAESAREAN SECTIONS

It is important to know just when it is needed, and not to panic yourself into a Caesar. When is a Caesar necessary? A puppy may be too big (often when the bitch only has one or two puppies). A puppy may be wrongly presented, 'jamming up' all the puppies behind. Sometimes in very large litters, even in the bigger breeds, a bitch may just tire, after

perhaps having seven or eight pups quite normally, and a Caesar may be necessary to deliver the last-comers. A bitch which has a particularly small pelvis, or which has suffered an accident such as a broken pelvis, will need veterinary guidance and most probably a Caesarean in order to whelp. Talk this over with your vet before you mate her.

Uterine inertia is quite common in some breeds. This does run in families. Quite honestly, it is wise never to keep a female puppy for breeding who has been whelped from such a bitch. It's better to be on the safe side and establish a good, strong whelping bitch line, going on generation after generation. Sometimes, in the case of uterine inertia, a Caesarean can be avoided and labour can be induced by injections administered by the vet.

There are also what are known as 'elective' Caesareans – when the pregnancy is planned, knowing that the bitch will have a Caesarean operation to have her litter. This is sometimes done with bitches which have had trouble in the past, or when difficulties are likely for some reason or another, for instance a damaged pelvis or repaired uterine inertia. The operation is generally performed a few days before the due date. This is quite acceptable. On the other hand, it is not acceptable for breeders to use a Caesarean for their own convenience if they want to go to a dog show, or all sorts of frivolous excuses. It is a major operation, after all.

How do you know when your bitch needs a Caesar, especially if she is a maiden bitch, or has previously whelped successfully? Here is yet another reason for constant supervision. A whelping bitch must be watched. No need to hang over her, fussing her and yourself – just quiet steady supervision is required. If more than two hours of straining elapse, get in touch with your vet at once. Have a chat to your vet about the type of anaesthetic used. Most vets these days can use gas for small or medium-size breeds. This is (from experience) marvellous – the bitch comes round very quickly. If the other type of anaesthetic is used, probably more time will elapse before your girlie really comes around. Your bitch will be groggy for some time. Do not put the puppies straight in with her, especially if she is a maiden. She will not know quite what has happened to her, and still being not quite 'with us', will possibly squash them. Keep them apart for a few hours. However, do make sure that they obtain the colostrum (i.e. 'first milk') from her after an hour or two has elapsed. She may get the whole idea and start nuzzling and cleaning them, but, to avoid possible losses, keep the puppies away from her until she has completely come round. Make sure that the bitch is warm, and whatever you do, keep her quiet. Resist the temptation to let friends and family see her and the new litter, however hard they beg. It is better to have just one person tending to her, although when you are dead tired (especially if you have to feed the babies for a couple of days and nights), it's a good idea to have a back-up helper. No more than one!

THE NEWBORN LITTER
Check the puppies for obvious defects such as cleft palates. Puppies will drink from the bitch in one hour or sooner. They are very quick to find the teat and will suckle vigorously, and it is essential they get the colostrum, the first milk, which contains antibodies from the mother. Make sure the bitch is taken outside to urinate; it is hard for her to feed puppies with a full bladder. Watch your bitch and puppies carefully for the first weeks, and if they show any signs of fading, consult your vet immediately. Puppies should always feel warm. If you find that one puppy is not receiving a fair share at the milk bar, you will need to help. Hold the puppy firmly in your hand and place the puppy on to a teat. You might have to express some milk to encourage the little one to take hold. Keep the puppy there until some food has been taken. Remember a puppy has a very small stomach, so it will not take long before it is full.

Make sure the puppies' nails are kept short to prevent them scratching their mother while feeding. It is good practice to place the puppies on their backs on your knee occasionally, with their hind legs towards you, so that you can check the claws and feet. Use either a small sharp pair of scissors, or the human nail clippers, and just trim the end off each claw. This position is also very useful when grooming the underside of the mature dog. Remember to talk quietly to the pup as you go along. The mother will not like you doing this, so sit next to the whelping box so she can see what you are doing, or wait until the mother has gone out to relieve herself, and then check them. This is also the ideal time to replace any soiled papers and bedding. You could check the babies over and weigh them at the same time. Their mother will wash each pup when she returns to remove your scent. Leave the mother with her puppies for as long as she is happy. They learn such a lot from her.

HANDFEEDING THE PUPPIES
These days there are many different formulas for feeding and practically

everyone has their own ideas. If you are stuck, use mine – many, many puppies have been reared on it and it could not be more simple – 8 oz. evaporated milk (for example, Carnation), 8 oz. water, 6 vitamin drops (we use Pentavite), 6 drops gripe water. Feed from the smallest baby's bottle you can get. We never had any luck with the tiny bottles sold for small-breed puppy nursing. We found that, even in the smallest breeds, the puppies' mouths would open wide enough for a baby teat. Get one with a small hole to start with, enlarging it as puppy grows. Tube feeding is not as popular as it used to be. We do not like it at all, preferring, especially with very weak puppies, to dropper-feed until they are strong enough to suckle.

How often do you feed? Again from our own experience, every two hours for the first two days, then every two hours during the day, every three hours at night. Break the feeds down to every three hours during the day, last feed at midnight, then again at six o'clock in the morning. With very small puppies, you might still need a middle-of-the-night feed. If the puppies are warm, growing and content, be guided by this. Let the mother see you feeding them. At first, while she is not up to things, you will gently have to stimulate the puppies' bodily functions (use a damp piece of cotton wool for this and imitate the licking action of the mother), but as soon as the mother starts cleaning them up, you can relax a little. Usually, after about twenty-four hours, the mother has completely taken over and you can start to enjoy your litter!

THE FIRST WEEKS

Do not forget that the pups need to have their tails docked and dewclaws cut at three to four days old. The tail should be docked at one-eighth of an inch above the tan on the underside of the tail. Silky Terrier pups are born black and tan with a smooth coat like satin; their eyes open at ten to fourteen days. Their eyes will appear cloudy at first. This will clear as they are able to focus and see clearly. Their ears will be opening also at this time. For the first three weeks of their life the mother will give them all the nourishment they require. The bitch should have two main meals of fresh red meat, mixed with a good canned meat, plenty of warm milk, eggs, cheese, fish and vegetable and syrup. It is most important to ensure that the bitch always has fresh cold water; this will help keep her milk supply up. In a few weeks your puppies will be on their feet, and very playful. Silky puppies are little explorers, wandering round their box quite early in life. Make sure you have provided blankets over the newspapers to give them a firm footing. A small area in front of their whelping box, and at floor level, needs to be arranged so that they can toddle and roll around. They will soon learn to relieve themselves in the play area. Put down clean newspaper – maybe a dozen times a day. It is safer to shut them in their bed at night, as they need to be kept warm.

WEANING

At about three weeks it is time for the bitch to be taken away from the puppies for a few hours each day. This is when the fun starts. Now is the time to start feeding the puppies. You can use the following diet for very young puppies: half a tin of Carnation Milk, the yolk of one egg, one teaspoon of calcium supplement, half a cup of baby's cereal, four drops of Pentavite, 2.5 ml. of gripe water and half a cup of boiling water, all mixed into a thin creamy consistency.

Alternatively, and much more conveniently, there are some very good commercial puppy foods available from your vet or pet stores. These have been specially made and contain all the necessary vitamins and minerals required by puppies. Most of these just require you to add some cooled, boiled water. There is a puppy Formula on the market which mixes to make a soft consistency, and then it can be made thicker, into a porridge. Start your puppies, one at a time, to take a sip from a teaspoon or dropper. Begin feeding this milk mixture morning and night, and at lunch time give about two teaspoons of good raw mince beef, which has had a little boiled water poured over it and been allowed to cool, or soaked completed puppy meal which is prepared for this purpose. The bitch will be only too happy to clean her puppies between meals, and to sleep with them. Gradually increase the quantity as the puppies grow, add a little cheese or fish, and one more main meal.

THE DEVELOPING LITTER

The puppies are now six weeks old, time for needles and the visit to your vet. There is a golden rule – always hold your puppies for the needle, so that they will not be frightened of the judging table when the times comes to show them. By this time the puppies are having six small meals a day and mum only comes to clean them up. Remember, they are still very small puppies, and their stomachs can only digest small amounts, so it is better to feed small meals often. As the puppies grow, enlarge their run to enable them to play and exercise themselves. Should you have a very small pup in your litter, it is often necessary to separate this one from the others, who can get rough and injury may occur. The puppies by now will be able to have a run and play with their mother. Some bitches, when their milk has gone, will regurgitate their last meal into the bed for their offspring. Keeping her from the pups until sometime after her meal, and feeding the pups just before she returns, may help. It's only nature at work, and there is no use scolding her, and it will do no harm to the pups. By this time your pups should have been wormed four times with a good worming syrup (ask your vet for a syrup suitable for small puppies) and had their six/seven weeks needle (do not forget your puppies' vet vaccination card).

SELLING THE PUPPIES

By now your puppies' registration papers should be back from your Kennel Club. The big day comes for your puppies to leave: some breeders are glad to see them go – no more mess to clean up – but deep down it is a time when one feels a sense of loss because, after helping these puppies into the world, and rearing them for eight weeks or more, they feel part of your home. When people come to take their puppies they are excited. Have a few small boxes ready, and some old clean towels, for the puppies to travel in. These are things the new owner tends to forget. Remember to hand over: the puppy's pedigree; the puppy's vaccination certificate; notes on coat care and grooming; a diet sheet; your phone number; two or three meals; and a few heartworm tablets (if applicable).

10 *HEALTH CARE*

It must be emphasised that this is a *guide* to the health care of your Silky. It is in no way meant to discourage any owner, who has the slightest doubt about the condition of their dog, from seeking the advice of a vet. It is meant to help you assess the seriousness of certain symptoms and conditions, and give practical advice on what to do until the vet arrives, or until you get to a vet, and what ailments you can treat yourself. A sick dog will usually look or act differently. The common signs include some, or all, of the following: running eyes; refusing food; a dull coat; vomiting; the dog feeling warm to touch; a dry nose; continuous scratching; the dog shaking its head; the dog dragging itself around on its backside; the dog wanting to drink constantly; and diarrhoea or an obvious discharge.

Marshdae Whata Chance To Dream, aged ten months. The Silky is generally a fit breed and should experieince few major health problems.

Photo: Russell Fine Art.

A TO Z OF COMMON AILMENTS

ABSCESSES

An abscess is a localised collection of pus accompanied by swelling and inflammation. Usually this swelling increases to a head, then the abscess softens, then bursts. *Do not squeeze* the abscess, as you will do more harm than good. Bathe it using one cup of warm water with salt or a mild antiseptic solution added to it. If the abscess does not burst within two days, please consult your vet, who will have to lance it, and follow this treatment with a course of antibiotics. A vet should also be consulted if the abscess is caused by tooth decay.

ANAL GLANDS

If a dog smells offensively and continually rubs its backside along the ground this is usually the sign that the anal glands need to be cleared. Squeeze firmly, but carefully, against the base of the anal glands. When clearing the anal glands an offensive smelly discharge will be released, so you will need to have something like an old towel in your hands, in which to catch it. When embarking on this for the first time, it is best to get an experienced breeder, or your vet, to show you how to do it.

ARTIFICIAL RESPIRATION (CPR)

Canine CPR (Cardio Pulmonary Resuscitation) should be administered as soon as breathing stops. A delay of even three minutes may be fatal. Place the animal on the right side, open the mouth and remove any loose material that may impair breathing. Extend the tongue fully, place the palm of one hand over the ribs of the dog and the palm of the other hand under the shoulder. Compress gently but firmly: a quick depression is better than a shallow compression. Follow the natural rhythm of the heart. This should be repeated every four-and-a-half to five seconds until the animal starts to breathe regularly. This may take up to one hour.

For mouth to mouth resuscitation, place the dog's head in your hand and breathe into the dog's nostrils. Wait for one second, then blow again. Repeat this until the dog breathes again. If it is a puppy which is in difficulties, you could slap the pup once or twice on its side, then lift the pup by the hind legs and, with extended arms, swing the puppy to and fro about eight to ten times. If breathing does not commence after three to four sessions of swings, try mouth to mouth resuscitation. *IMPORTANT: If breathing has stopped due to an electric shock, make sure you turn the power off at source first.*

BAD BREATH

As a rule, a dog with bad breath is not well. If the condition persists for more than forty-eight hours, go to your vet for advice. In a puppy under eight months of age, bad breath sometimes accompanies the teething stage. It also could be a good indication that the puppy needs worming. With more mature dogs, bad breath may indicate a number of diseases such as tonsillitis, a stomach infection, ulcers of the mouth, infected or broken teeth, labial eczema (a condition of the lips), or sinusitis. With older dogs, continuing bad breath may indicate a degree of chronic kidney failure. If all other diseases have been checked out and you have the all-clear, you can try charcoal tablets – dosage one tablet per 4.5 kg. (10 lb) about one to six times a day.

BITES AND STINGS

Snake and spider bites are treated in the

or a twitching face; and the dog will run in short, apparently mindless, circles

EARS AND EYES

The most common ear problem is canker. The primary symptoms include: a build-up of wax; parasites; ruptured blood vessels; inflammation of the cartilage and canal; an offensive discharge; repeated shaking of the head; continuous scratching; and the dog holding the head to one side. Cleaning of the ears with cotton wool buds and an antiseptic, or ear cleaner, should ease the problem. *Important: do not poke* the cotton bud in the ear when cleaning, you could burst the ear drum. If the problem persists, see your vet. The secondary symptoms include loss of balance and the dog can die. The most common eye disease is conjunctivitis. Bathe the eyes frequently with a recommended solution in the early stages. If it persists, see your vet.

FLEAS

Fleas on dogs must not be tolerated. If unchecked, they can lead to more serious infection, and hair loss is great. They can destroy the best-coated dogs. Prevention is better than a cure. You can go to your vet's clinic and obtain one of the many effective powders, sprays and dog collars available for the inquiring owner. Do not overlook the dog's sleeping area and bedding. *Make sure it is kept clean and dry, and is regularly disinfected.*

GRASS EATING

Why do dogs eat grass? Because they have a sore stomach, so eating grass will not hurt them, it just sweetens the stomach.

HEPATITIS

Canine Hepatitis is a disease of dogs characterised by a loss of appetite, depression, diarrhoea often with blood, tonsillitis and acute abdominal pain, due to enlargement of the liver. The disease may be severe, with death occurring within 24 to 36 hours of its onset, or mild, with the dog only showing signs of loss of appetite and general lethargy. Corneal opacity (a cloudy-looking eye) which is often known as 'blue eye' may follow the infection. This will need treatment from the vet.

KENNEL COUGH

Kennel cough (Infectious Tracheo-bronchitis) is a contagious disease of dogs which has more than one cause. Affected dogs have a hacking cough, which usually appears after exercise, and may persist for several weeks. Among the infectious agents associated with kennel cough are a bacterium and two viruses. Treatment with antibiotics sometimes speeds recovery. Affected dogs frequently have been resident in a boarding kennel, training complex, or veterinary hospital, or have been in close contact with other dogs at shows, racetracks, obedience classes or similar assemblies, within the previous five to ten days. Vaccination is the best method of control.

MILK FEVER

See Chapter 9: Whelping and Rearing.

NAILS

Clipping nails. If the nail is black and the quick cannot be seen, cut along the line formed by the end of the nail level with the paw. Do not cut the nail too short or you will cut into the quick (vein) under the nail and may cause bleeding. Long nails can cause weak pasterns and lameness.

PARVOVIRUS

Canine Parvovirus is a disease of dogs of all ages but especially young pups. Death can occur within 24 hours of the onset of illness. The usual signs of infection are listlessness or depression followed by vomiting and blood-stained diarrhoea. Serious dehydration often results. Without treatment many dogs will die, but even with treatment a significant number of dogs can still die. The best defence is inoculation against the disease.

PULSE

For a Toy dog the average pulse rate is approximately 100 beats per minute. You can read the pulse by placing your two fingers on the inside of the rear hind leg. The rate may increase during illness to approximately 150 beats per minute, but sometimes it may decrease slightly.

SUNSTROKE AND HEAT EXHAUSTION

This is very common in the summer months when dogs are locked in cars or kept in the sun too long. The symptoms are: heavy panting; dullness; stumbling; and sweating through the footpads. If the body temperature rises to 43 degrees Celsius the dog will collapse and die. The treatment is to cool the animal quickly: give the dog water to drink and make more available; sponge the dog down if possible, if not use a hose. If the condition is more serious, apply ice packs to the body, especially the head and chest. Keep giving the dog water, to overcome dehydration.

TEMPERATURE

The body temperature of a dog should normally be between 38.3 and 38.7 degrees Celsius (100.7 and 101.9 degrees Fahrenheit). The temperature is normally taken by placing a round-nosed thermometer in the rectum. Lubricate it with Vaseline first. In a non-whelping situation a temperature of 102 F would indicate ill health.

TICKS

If a tick is found, kill it by applying kerosene, turpentine or methylated spirits, and remove it. If you are unable to kill it, lever it out carefully with a pair of sharp-pointed scissors, keeping the head intact. Avoid pulling on the tick with tweezers: it could cause more poison to be injected into the dog. Alternatively, cover the tick with vaseline, which will cut off its oxygen supply and it will then drop off intact. Symptoms of the presence of a tick are: pain at the site of bite; swelling and redness around the bite; nausea or vomiting; and a change in the dog's bark to a cough. *Important:* the dog could develop tick paralysis, in which case go to your vet immediately.

WORMS

Worms are common in all dogs and more so in puppies. The symptoms are: a pot belly; the dog vomiting worms; worms in the faeces; worms can interfere with normal growth rate; loss of appetite; dullness of coat; and breaking hair. Treatment involves buying worming syrups or tablets from your vet. You can also go onto a worming programme from your vet. There is one worm that can be transmitted to humans – roundworm. So educate children and adults to wash their hands after playing with your pet. A good idea is to worm your family at the same time as your animals.

FIRST AID KIT

A First Aid Kit should be on hand at all times. In your kit you should have:

A pair of sharp scissors
A pair of blunt scissors
Tweezers
4 Rolls 2 inch (5 cm) Elastoplast
4 Rolls 2 inch (5 cm) Roller Bandage
Cotton Wool and Cotton Buds
Bottle Hydrogen Peroxide
Bottle Antiseptic or Dettol
A needle
Paracetamol Tablets
Milk of Magnesia and Charcoal Tablets
Eyedropper
Vinegar or 'Stingo'
Cold compress
Thermometer
Vaseline.

CARE OF THE OLDER DOG

A little extra care and thought can make the later years of your dog's life just as happy and enjoyable for you both as those of puppyhood and the middle years. Elderly dogs, like elderly people, come in all shapes and sizes, and like people, the behaviour of one dog may be very different to that of another. A dog of only five or six years may display elderly behaviour patterns, while another of thirteen or fourteen continues to exhibit a youthful joy in living. The first signs of ageing may be a greying of the muzzle, a general slowing down and a slight stiffening of the joints, which results in the dog rising or lying down more slowly and carefully. Your dog may show an increased interest in the dinner bowl, but for the sake of the health of your dog, resist those pleading eyes. Being overweight puts a strain on the heart, on the joints and on the digestion. If the dog is already overweight, now is the time to reduce the food intake until the correct weight is reached. Some dogs will continue to thrive on their usual diet, but others will benefit from lighter food – chicken, fish, scrambled egg and a finer grade of biscuit meal. If the dog's diet has been one of the complete foods, many of the manufacturing companies have one specially formulated for the older dog. Your dog may also cope better with two or three small meals a day, rather than one or two larger ones as previously given.

Perhaps one of the most crucial things in considering elderly dogs is to continue to make them feel needed and important, especially if there are younger dogs in the household. Though their reactions and their thoughts may be slower, they will enjoy a game several times a day to stimulate their mind and movement. Exercise needs to be tailored to the dog's general condition and willingness. If the dog is fit and obviously enjoying the daily walks, then by all means continue them, but it is cruel to force a reluctant and distressed old dog to walk the miles the dog enjoyed when young. Several short walks to stimulate circulation and interest may suit better.

Grooming should become a more gentle event, with a softer brush and a lighter touch. Old bones may ache and old muscles may be sore. A six-monthly veterinary check, rather than an annual one, is well worth considering. The vet will be able to make an early diagnosis of any medical or dental problems which may be developing. The elderly dog appreciates warmth and should be dried well after being out on a wet day. Ensure that the dog always goes to bed warm and dry. The elderly dog will also appreciate peace and privacy, and will welcome a safe haven from where it is possible see what it going on, but which is out of the reach of the children and any other dogs or puppies in the household.

Some elderly dogs become incontinent. This usually takes the form of a little leaking while the dog is deeply asleep. The dog may be unaware of what has happened and for the sake of maintaining your dog's dignity, any such accidents are best ignored. Deafness affects most elderly dogs to a greater or lesser degree. It may be necessary to touch the dog to rouse him from sleep. It can be useful to teach your dog to respond to a few hand signals if your commands can no longer be heard. The dog's eyes may look 'milky', indicating that cataracts are forming and the dog will see less clearly. The loss of hearing and sight are gradual processes and dogs adapt remarkably well. Neither disability is a reason for putting them to sleep.

Ideally, all dogs would die in their sleep, but this is quite rare. It is more usual for the owner to have to make the difficult decision that the dog's life is no longer a happy one, and to ask the vet to give the final injection which sends the dog peacefully and painlessly into permanent sleep. When the time comes, do stay with your old friend while the injection is given – harrowing though it is, it is a small price to pay for all the years of pleasure your dog has given you. If possible, allow any other dogs you have to see their friend so that they do not seek him in the next few days. All animals understand death, and it is less distressing for them and for you if they are aware of your dog's passing. It is perfectly normal and natural to grieve for the loss of a dog. Owners sometimes feel disloyal about bringing a new puppy into the household after the loss of an elderly dog. A new puppy takes up so much time that this does help to soften the loss. The old dog is not forgotten, but it is less painful when there is less time to grieve. Every dog is different, and each will be loved for themselves as they take up their own place in the household.

11. THE SILKY IN AUSTRALIA AND NEW ZEALAND

Being a true Australian, the Silky can be found all over the country. Here is a State-by-State guide to the Australian Silky in its homeland.

THE AUSTRALIAN CAPITAL TERRITORY (CANBERRA)

The ACT formed a Club in the 1950s named The Australian Silky Terrier and Yorkshire Terrier Club. This Club holds two Championship Shows each year, always well run. Early Breeders were Mrs Ann Elford – Australian Silky and Yorkshire Terrier (Booroondara Kennels), Mr Cyril Lancaster (Kabakaul Kennels), Mrs Elaine Nugent – Australian Silky and Yorkshire Terrier (Coolibah Kennels), the Sutton family (Delbrae Kennels) and Mr and Mrs A. Reeves (Demilo Kennels). Many ACT Silkies have been top winners. To name just a few: Sutton's Ch. Delbrae Tiny Contessa, Mrs Meyer's Ch. Delbrae Capt. Starlite CD, Mrs E. Nugent's Ch. Rodleen Major Max, and Mr and Mrs A. Reeves' Ch. Demilo Bobby Blue. Over the last ten years or so the number of exhibits at the Club's shows has dropped to half.

NEW SOUTH WALES

One of the early breeders in Sydney was Mr Tom Neeves. His Newton dogs were more uniform, a little bigger in size. Tom Neeves won The Prince of Wales Trophy three times in succession with Newton colours. The trophy was donated by Messrs. Brigment, McDonald and Moss to encourage the new breed. Some Newton dogs can still be found on many pedigrees today. Early breeders included Mr and Mrs D. Mace (Araluen Kennels), Mrs Page (Ellwyn Kennels), Mrs Milner (Aldoon Kennels), Mrs Birkin O'Donnell and Mr O'Donnell (Stroud Totham Kennels), Mrs T. Risdale (Prairie Kennels) and Mr Payne (Kendoral Kennels). Over the years we have had many dedicated followers conscious of their responsibility in breeding this great little dog to its true Standard. Many still flout the rules just for profit, but really the Australian Silky has come of age, and certainly today the breed makes its presence felt in the show ring, with many top awards.

During the last twenty-five years, we have seen many top-bred Australian Silkies in New South Wales. I could not name them all but I have selected a few special ones.

Ch. Valanne Sir Lancelot, bred and owned by the late Mrs Anne Richardson, was a delightful dog of good quality with a dark blue coat and rich tan. His awards included Group and In Show winner, Royal Challenges Sydney and Adelaide and Best in Show at The Australian Silky Terrier Club of NSW 1970. He was one of the top sires. Ch. Waiton Tiny Thumbelina was bred by Mrs R. Maher and owned by Mr and Mrs C.M. Parbery. She was a very smart bitch, winning Royal Challenges, Specialty Shows and many Group and In Show Awards. Ch. Koolamina Kiwi, bred by Mr Patterson and owned Mr and Mrs E. Watts was a very nice standard size with a Silver Blue topknot, a good showman and Group winner.

Ch. Waiton Carbon Copy, bred by Mrs R. Maher and owned Mrs K. Boyce, was a nice size and of good quality, with a good blue coat and nice rich tan. This Silky is one of New South Wales' top Champion winners, with three Specialty shows 1973, 74, 76, Best in Show, and, in 1981, went Best Opposite Sex in Show. Many Group and Best in Show wins added to a super career. Ch. Lylac Merry Minx To, bred and owned by Mrs Nancy Glynn, was a bitch of very good quality with outstanding coat, colour and tan, and one of the top winning bitches in the 1970s. Her achievements included the Sydney Royal Challenge, two Specialty Best in Shows, five Best Opposite Sex in Shows, and four Runner Up to Best in Show. This bitch must go down as one of the greats.

Ch. Valanne Sir Richard was bred and owned by Anne Richardson. This dog, to me, was one of the best, with a great ability to show. Without any disrespect to the owner and handler, if he had been shown by some of the handlers of today, he would have achieved far more in the show ring. He was a true terrier, well put together, with a good topline and sound all round, with good colour. His honours included Sydney Royal Challenge, Specialty Show, five Best in Shows all breeds, and many Group wins. He has also sired many Champions. Ch. Idem Eloise was bred and owned Mr and Mrs D. Hingeley. She was a bitch of excellent type, with a good blue coat colour, of standard size, well-bodied, sound all round and moved really well. Elly was a true terrier, which is very hard to find in bitches. Her achievements included Royal Challenges – Sydney 1980 and 81, Perth 1980, 81 and 82 and National Capital 1980; Opposite Sex in Toy Group Perth Royal 1980 and 81; New Zealand KC National Best of Breed 1978; Best in Show Specialty Shows, Best in Show All Breeds and many Best in Group wins. She was a top-class bitch.

Ch. Tarawera Pippin, who was bred by Miss N. Wren and owned Mr and Mrs D. Hingeley, was a true terrier – Mister Showman himself. This dog loved showing. He was an outstanding dog with good temperament, nice size, good blue coat and rich tan. In New South Wales he was the one and only Australian Silky to gain his Championship with only five challenges. Royal Challenges – Sydney 1979, Perth 1981, 82 and 84, and National Capital 1980. Best in Show – ASTC of NSW three in a row 1978-79, Victoria 1979, Perth 1982. Best in Shows All Breeds and many Best in Group awards. In 1979 Pip achieved over one week what no other Silky Terrier has done – BOB Sydney Royal, Best in Show 4P's All Toy Dog Club NSW, and ASTC of NSW. At the first Contest of Winners in Sydney, Pip was the first Silky, and one of three top winning toy dogs, to

Aust. Ch. Idem Eloise (Aust. Ch. Demilo Bobby Blue – Tarawera Mandy).

Aust. Ch. Tarawera Pippin, pictured with some of his trophies.

be invited. Pippin's last challenge and BOB was at Perth Royal 1984 – he was nine years old. A fine Champion.

Ch. Adamanda Carrie, bred by Miss R. Bennett, owned by Mr and Mrs T. Coombe, was a very smart, good-size bitch, always alert, with good movement, and sound. Best in Show ASTC of NSW April 1982 and April 1983, she was a nice bitch. Aust. NZ Ch. Tarawera Coolhand Luke, bred by Miss N. Wren and owned by the late Mr and Mrs R. Hitchens, was a nice type, an alert showy dog, with a light blue coat, nice tan. Luke did well as a young dog and gained his Championship at 11 months of age. Then after one year out of the show ring with heartworm he continued to do well in Australia and New Zealand, with many Group wins, one Best in Show and R/Up in show ASTC of NSW 1982 and 83, and Best in Show NSW Toy Show. Aust. NZ Ch. Bams Boy of Lakemba

Aust. N.Z. Ch. Bams Boy Of Lakemba (Wilsight Bam Bam – Aust. N.Z. Ch. Adamanda Honey Luv

Photo: Trafford.

Aust. Ch. Tarawera Emmancipation.

(Imp. NZ), was bred in New Zealand by R.A. McKay and owned by Miss R. Bennett. He was a good-bodied dog, with a coat of good blue with nice tan, and sound. He had many All Breed show wins – Sydney Royal Challenge 1984, Best in Show ASTC of NSW April and September 1984, March and September 1986 and September 1987. He also had many Best in Group awards. A dog to remember.

Ch. Tarawera Emancipation was bred and owned by Miss Wren, and was a winner from a baby. At her first Sydney Royal she was Reserve Challenge bitch from the Puppy Class, and at Perth Royal Challenge Bitch at just eleven months and Opposite Sex in Group at the same show. At the ACT Silky Show she was Challenge bitch and Junior in Show, 1984 Australian Silky Terrier NS. She was also Challenge bitch

Aust. Ch. Guruga
Julie Kent (Aust. Ch.
Demilo Bobby Blue –
Aust Ch. Keeshee
Misty Blue).

Photo: T. Dorizas.

Aust. N.Z. Ch.
Kamaroon of
Kelabrae (Aust.
N.Z. Ch. Tarawera
My Steel Dan –
Kelbrae Sheeza
Hijinks).

Photo: T. Dorizas.

Aust. N.Z. Guruga
Toucho Blue (Aust.
Sing. Ch. Hijack Of
Kelbrae – Aust .Ch.
Keeshee Misty Blue).

and Runner Up and Opposite Sex in Show. She is a very sound bitch with good movement, and light blue coat and tan. She is all terrier and one of our top dams.

Ch. Guruga Julie Kent was bred by Mrs J. Walker and is owned Miss Wren. Julie is always the lady, a delightful bitch with a lovely head and eyes, good movement and great temperament, along with a good blue coat and rich tan. She is a Royal Challenge winner, and one Best in Show, with many Class in Group wins. This bitch is a very lovely girl.

Aust. NZ Ch. Guruga Toucho Blue, was bred Mrs J. Walker, owned again by Miss Wren. Didja, as she is affectionately named, is a delightful bitch of standard size and good quality, with a lovely fine silky blue coat and nice tan. She has had Royal Challenges in National Capital, Sydney and Brisbane. She has 72 Toy Groups to her name, and many In Group and In Show awards, plus one Runner up at a Specialty Club Show. She is a first class bitch. Aust. NZ Ch. Kamaroon of Kelbrae (Imp. NZ) was bred in New Zealand from Australian bloodlines by Mrs A. Crenfeldt and is owned by Crenfeldt, Scales and Wren. This exciting young dog has certainly taken over the Toy ring. He is a sturdily constructed dog with strong terrier character in alertness and soundness, together with a lovely dark blue coat and rich tan, good head and ears, and good movement. Kamaroon has had 45 Best Exhibit in Shows, and five Australian Silky Terrier NSW Specialty Shows, and one Specialty show in the ACT, plus 53 Runner Up in Shows, Best Exhibit in Groups, and Class in Show awards All Breeds. He was Top Toy in NSW 1994 at only four years of age. He is a remarkable Silky with many years ahead of him, and is a top sire with

Champions in five states of Australia. To date Kamaroon is the most awarded Silky in Australia and New Zealand – we know of no other in the world to have been awarded 45 Best in Shows.

VICTORIA

The names of Mr Rowe, Mr Leggo, Mr Keyser, Mrs Grieveson and Mr Bonneti are accredited with taking honours for the Silky Coated Terriers. These breeders were the pioneers of the Silky Coated Terriers in Victoria. Top winning Silky Terriers at this stage included Caroustic Jack, Benny, Trilby's Daughter, Jess, Crescent Bluebell, Tarago Dolly and Rebellion. When the 1939/45 war ended there was a surge of interest in dog showing and, with travel becoming easier, the sport of dog showing took off. Into this era came well-known breeders such as Mrs J. Wenker, Hillside (Ch. Hillside Peter Pan and Ch. Hillside Select); A. Miles, Milan (Ch. Milan Tony and Ch. Milan Vanessa); V. Fitch, Tamworth (Ch. Tamworth Gay Spark and Ch. Tamworth Nikki); Mr E. Fellows, Bowenvale (Ch. Bowenvale Sir Rex and Ch. Bowenvale Murray); Mr D. Blewett, Rodleen (Ch. Rodleen Salient and Ch. Rodleen Dameeli); Mrs Collins, Collinvale (Ch. Collinvale Penelope); Mrs V. Clarke, Kateena (Ch. Kateena Thor and Ch. Kateena Deborah); and E. Reid, Bogunda (Ch. Bogunda Panitya and Ch. Bogunda Boy Blue). There were so many breeders showing during the period from 1940 to the present day, that it is impossible to mention them all. Now there are newer breeder/showers entering the ring alongside the 'old' ones and we can only hope that they can go into the future with confidence with this little breed, the Australian Silky Terrier, that has evolved

*Aust. Ch. Balkana
Front Page News.*

over the last 100 years to what it is today.

Ch. Karribi Blue Glen, bred and owned by J. and J. Geoghegan, was a sound dog with a good-texture light blue coat, of a nice size, with nice dark eyes and a good expression and good movement. He won Royal Challenges in most States of Australia and was Best in Show, Australian Silky Terrier Club of Victoria 1975 and 76, Best in Group and In Show winner. He was one of Victoria's top sires at that time. Ch. Karribi Blue Gem, also bred and owned by J. and J. Geoghegan, and litter sister to Ch. Karribi Blue Glen, was a very feminine bitch of good class, nice size, good light blue coat with nice tan, and sound all round. She had Royal Challenges and many Group wins. Ch. Kaylaw Tinka Bell, bred and owned by Mrs K. McGregor, was a delightful bitch with a lovely blue coat and good tan, nice head and ears, good movement and topline, and had Royal Challenges Victoria 1979 and 80 to her credit. Ch. Kaylaw Letem Talk, also bred and owned by Mrs McGregor, is a very showy dog with a good-coloured blue coat, and nice tan. He is the winner of four Victoria Silky Shows, 1985, 86, 87 and 89, and Royal Challenges 1985 and 88, plus

many in Group and In Show wins. He is a dog to remember. Kaylaw Kennels have been one of Victoria's top Silky kennels over many years, with Tinka Bell, Letem Talk, Ch. Kaylaw Kansas and Ch. Kaylaw Whata Nuisance all being Royal Challenge winners.

Ch. Allanette Valentino, bred and owned by Mrs A. Collins, is a nice alert dog of good size, type and colour. He has a good strong topline, is true in movement, well trained and always nicely presented. His achievements include Royal Challenges Melbourne Royal 1989, Brisbane Royal 1989 and Runner Up in Toy Group, Victoria's Specialty Show Best in Show 1988 and Best in Show All Breeds. Other top dogs from Allanette Kennels are Ch. Allanette Miss Muffet and Ch. Allanette Super Brat. Ch. Balkana Front Page News is bred and owned by Mr J. Camac. Aged two-and-a-half years, he is the new kid on the block in Victoria. He is a very alert young dog, with good expression, ear-set and lovely reach of neck, excellent blue colour and tan. He is a Multiple Best Exhibit in Group winner and looking forward to a bright career.

123

*Aust. Ch.
Dulcannina Robbie:
A proiific show
winner.*

*Photo:
K. Barkleigh-Shute.*

*Aust. Ch.
Dulcannina
Laramie.*

SOUTH AUSTRALIA

In South Australia the Silky was first shown by a Mr T. Bourke in 1919. Challenges were awarded from 1924, with Mr Bennett's Durham Kennels taking a major share of the awards. To date there is no Breed Club in South Australia. Most of the top dogs in South Australia have been from one kennel.

Aust. NZ Ch. Dulcannina Robbie, bred and owned by Mrs F. Camac, was a cobby dog with good terrier head and excellent topline, and a light blue coat, nice tan. Robbie was the first Silky to win a Best Exhibit in Show in New Zealand. Winner of two Best Exhibit in Show Auckland All Breeds; Best in Show Silky Club of Victoria 1977, and Opposite Sex in Show in 1978 and numerous Best in Group awards, plus four consecutive Melbourne Royal

Aust. Ch. Dulcannina Christel.

Aust. Ch. Dulcannina To The Max (S.A. N.Z. Ch. Kamaroon of Kelbrae – Aust. Ch. Ensta Fancy Freeby).

Photo: Cabal.

Challenges 1974, 75, 76 and 77 and Adelaide Royal Challenge winner 1974, 75 & 77, he was a big winner at a time when Australian Silky Terriers were not considered for high awards. Another Champion bred and owned by Mrs Camac was Ch. Dulcannina Kansas, who made history by winning Best in Show at Melbourne Royal Centenary 1972. He was a nice size, with dark blue coat and rich tan. He showed and moved well. His Challenges were Melbourne Royal 1972 and Adelaide Royal 1972 & 73 and he was the sire of eleven Champions. Ch. Dulcannina Laramie was another success for Mrs Camac. A nice sound dog of good size and outline, with good type, temperament and movement and a nice dark blue coat, he was Adelaide Royal Challenge winner 1978 and 79; Best

Exhibit in Group Adelaide Royal 1979; Melbourne Royal Challenge 1979 and Sydney Royal Challenge and Best Exhibit in Toy Group. He also had many Best Exhibit in Group awards All Breeds and was a top winner for the Dulcannina Kennels.

Ch. Dulcannina Christel, again bred and owned by Mrs Camac, was a delightful bitch of good quality, nice size, very sound with good terrier head and well placed ears. She moved well, and possessed excellent temperament, a good blue coat and nice tan. Her achievements were two Best Exhibit in Shows and five Opposite Sex in Shows, including Victorian Silky Club Specialty Show, 16 Best Exhibit in Groups, 10 Best Opposite Sex in Groups, Adelaide Royal Challenge bitch 1973, 74 and 75, and Melbourne Royal 1975. A top bitch.

Ch. Ensta Fancy Freeby was also owned by Mrs Camac, together with Michael Camac, but bred by Mrs C. Borserio. Sasha, as she is called, did not know what a dog show was until relatively late in her life, and has she made up for it! – every bit a show girl who loves the show ring. She is a good-spirited bitch with a nice head and topline. She has excellent movement coming and going, a nice coat and rich tan and is well put together. This bitch is one of Dulcannina's bigger winners, with Royal Challenges in Adelaide, Sydney, Perth, & Darwin; numerous Best Exhibit in Show All Breeds and was Top Dog, South Australia 1994 and 95. She is a delightful bitch and a top dam. Ch. Dulcannina To The Max is bred and owned by Mrs and Mr Camac and is a son of Ch. Ensta Fancy Freeby. He is a nice-size, alert dog of good colour, with a true terrier head, tail just a little overgay, but overall very well put together. He has had many Best in Group

and In Show awards and is a Sydney and Perth Royal Challenge winner. He is still only a young dog – the best is yet to come.

QUEENSLAND

In Queensland the breed was known as a Sydney Silky as late as 1949. In 1987 a few Silky Terrier fanciers in Queensland, with a lot of hard work and dedication from its members, formed a social club, hoping to promote this great little terrier. In 1988 the Canine Control of Queensland granted Affiliation – The Australian Silky Terrier Club of Queensland was on its way, the hard work by a handful of devoted members had paid off. The Club now holds two shows per year, a Championship Show in September and an Open Show in March, with an average entry of about 25 to 35 exhibits. This Club is the only one to have printed two small books, one to help Pet and Show owners, the other book to help Trainee Judges. The Trainee Judges book has been used in most States of Australia, and it has met with great approval.

Early Breeders in Queensland include Mrs Jackson, Janela Kennels, Mrs E. Rich, Mrs M. Cassidy, Cassem Kennels, and Mr and Mrs B. Hamilton, Merrinah Kennels. Merrinah Kennels was the top winning kennel for many years with Ch. Merrinah Glens Lass and Ch. Merrinah Puff N Stuff, two very nice typey bitches with good coat, light blue and nice tan.

Ch. Silkreen Angelique, bred and owned by Mrs D. Dawson, Northern Queensland, is a nice-size bitch, light blue coat and nice tan. She is an In Show and In Group award winner. Ch. Myanchell Madonna, bred and owned by Mr and Mrs G. Rohde was a nice typey bitch of good size. Her show records are one Opposite Sex in Show and Intermediate in Show All Breeds with over

1,100 entries; Reserve and Opposite Sex in Show Australian Silky Terrier Club of Queensland 1985 and many Best Exhibit in Group and in Show awards. Ch. Myanchell Touch Oclass, also bred and owned by the Rohdes, is a son of Ch. Myanchell Madonna; with a good blue coat and good tan, he is a nice showy dog. He was Best Exhibit in Show Australian Silky Terrier Club of Queensland, and also the Open Show in 1988, plus one Best Exhibit in Show All Breeds. Another from the same kennel is Ch. Myanchell Watta Gal, a daughter of Madonna, and a delightful bitch of good type, good-colour coat and nice tan, and sound all round. She was Best Exhibit in Show at the Toy Dog Club of Queensland 1993, Best in Show, Australian Silky Terrier Club of Queensland 1991, and Best in Show Australian Silky Terrier

Aust. Ch. Merrinah Puff N Stuff.

Club of NSW 1993 – a very nice career.

Ch. Balkana Ringmaster, bred Mr J. Camac and owned by J. Camac and K. Rose is a dog of good size, nice blue coat

Aust. Ch. Myanchell Madonna (Karribi Stardust – Karribi Firedance).

Aust. Ch. Myanchell Touch Oclass (Aust. Ch. Kaylaw Letem Talk – Aust. Ch. Myanchell Madonna).

Aust. Ch. Myanchell Watta Gal (Aust. Ch. Kaylaw Letem Talk – Aust. Ch. Myanchell Madonna).

Photo: Marks.

Aust Ch. Mahald Shiloh Blue (Aust. Ch. Penannji Lucas – Aust. Ch. Threeways Susie Blue).

and good tan. Sound all round and good movement. Macka has just added to his show record Best in Show at Royal Agricultural Society of Queensland, Toowoomba Royal Show, entry 1,632 exhibits; Multi Best in Show winner; has won Toy Dog Club Point Score Queensland 1994 and 95 and, by coming Best in Show at The Australian Silky Terrier Club of Queensland Open Show is one of the few Silkies to win Best in Show at a Royal show in Australia.

Ch. Kelahleh Jasmyn, bred by Mrs H. Lechner and owned by Mrs C. Bromfield is a delightful bitch of good quality, light blue coat and nice tan. She has well-set ears and good dark eyes and is a good shower with several Best in Show and In Group wins. A top bitch, Jasmyn was shown in Northern Queensland and she was Top Toy for two years. Ch. Clonteque Beau Ben, bred and owned by Miss C. Magson was Best Exhibit in Show, Australian Silky Terrier and Yorkshire Terrier Club of ACT 1987;

Reserve Challenges Brisbane Royal; and has Best in Group awards and many Class in Group awards. Beau is a nice-size dog of good coat with good temperament and sound movement and a light blue coat and nice tan.

Ch. Mahald Shiloh Blue (Imp. NZ), bred by G. and C. Mold, owned by Mrs P. Prodger, is a very nice compact standard-size dog of good colour, very sound with nice, small ears and a good topline with nice temperament – all this and a good show record with many Best in Group and In Group awards, Best in Show All Breeds, Brisbane Royal Challenge and BOB 1991. Aust. NZ Ch. Tarawera Elly is bred and owned by Miss N. Wren who featured so often in the Champions of NSW. She is a nice alert bitch, very showy, with a blue coat with good tan. She gained her title at fourteen months; was Sydney Royal Reserve Challenge Bitch 1990 at only ten months; and Reserve Challenge bitch and Best in Show, Australian Silky Terrier Club of NSW 1991. She has many Class in Show wins and Best Exhibit in Groups to her name. Aust. NZ Ch. Tarawera My Steel Dan is also bred and owned by Miss Wren. He is a very sound dog all round, a true terrier, full of himself, with good temperament and movement. He has a light blue coat, good tan, and lovely head and good dark eyes. He is sire of Aust. NZ Ch. Kamaroon of Kelbrae. He was Top Australian Silky in New Zealand 1990 and 91; Best Exhibit in Show Australian Silky Terrier Club of NSW 1991; Best Exhibit in Open Show Australian Silky Terrier of Queensland 1991; Brisbane Royal Challenge winner 1990 and Reserve Challenge 1991 plus two Best Exhibit in Show at Toy Dog shows, multi in Show and In Group winner. He is one of the current top sires in Australia.

WESTERN AUSTRALIA

Some of the earliest records come from the 1919 Perth Royal. There were two classes: Australian Terrier Silky, Over 8 lbs. and Under 15 lbs. No challenge was issued. 1920 Perth Royal, no challenges issued. 1921 Perth Royal, Judge Mr E.C. Thomas. Australian Terrier Hard Coated, no challenge and Australian Terrier Silky Coated, challenge winner Sport Open Dog, S. Snooker and D. Peg O'My Heart, Breeder and Exhibitor T.H. Hart. One bitch – awarded 2nd Open Bitch class. Overall entry four, one puppy dog (B. Monison – Kalgoorlie) and two Open Dogs and one bitch (Mrs. Nolan). In 1935 they were shown at the Perth Royal as Silky Terriers. Also at this time breeders were permitted to register with a suffix and not a prefix. Also challenges were issued by the Western Australia Kennel Club, and did not become Australian National Champions

until a later date. After the 1940s some of the successful kennels were O. Taylor, Rodmaur, Juellen Kennels, Mrs Crawford, Glendower, Mrs D. McLean, Thackaringa, Mrs Clamp, Kingsley, Miss R. Shepherd, Norge, Mrs P. Byrne-King, Burnvale, Mr D. Westley, Tombeau and T. Hunter, Retnuh. In the late 1960s a breed club was formed under the name Australian Silky and Yorkshire Terrier Club of WA. This Club ceased operating in the mid 1980s because of insufficient interest amongst members. A new Club was formed in June 1992 under the name Australian Silky Terrier Club of WA. They held their first Championship Show in March, 1996.

Ch. Norge El Rajah 2nd, bred and owned by Miss R. Shepherd, was Challenge Dog Perth Royal in the 1960s. To date Rajah is the only Silky in Western Australia to have won five straight challenges at the Royal. Ch. Retnuh Ausytoo, bred by Mrs T. Hunter and owned Rosedale Kennels and Mrs N.F. Walker, is an excellent showman, with good movement and topline, a true terrier head with good expression and a light colour and tan. His achievements include Perth Royal challenge BOB 1988, 89 and 90. Sydney Royal BOB 1991 and numerous in Group and Class in Group awards. Ch. Parmelia Talk Up A Storm, bred and owned by J.L. Hickey and H.M. Horne, is a smart showman, with correct head and expression, light blue colour and tan. He is well-proportioned in accordance with his size, with overall soundness. He is a typical 'All Breeds Judge' type Australian Silky. He went Perth Royal Challenge BOB 1992 and 94, Runner Up Best in Group 1992; Western Classic Challenge BOB 1993, 94, 95 and 96; Runner Up Best in Group 1993 and was Top Winning Australian Silky of the

Aust. Ch. Kelbrae Rhubarb (Aust. N.Z. Ch. Kamaroon of Kelbrae – N.Z. Ch. Tarawera Charisma).

Tarawera Jeune (Aust. N.Z. Ch. Tarawera My Steel Dan – Aust.N.Z. Ch. Guruga Toucho Blue).

Year WA Point Score 1992. Ch. Kelbrae Rhubarb, bred by Mrs A. Crenfeldt (NZ) and owned by Mrs P. Hingeley, is a true terrier in every sense of the word, with an excellent topline on the move and while free-standing, and correct tail-set. He posseses overall soundness with good spring of rib and depth of chest, and a light blue colour with rich tan. Rhubarb gained his first Challenge at eight months of age, and was titled at 23 months of age. During these 15 months he was a Runner Up in Group winner, and titled with a Best Exhibit in Group; Best Exhibit in Show ASTC of NSW 1994; Best Exhibit in Show WA Toy Dog Specialist Club 1995 and 96; Best Exhibit in Show, All Breeds Western Australia and Queensland; Runner Up Top Toy of the Year WA 1994 and 95; Top Winning Australian Silky of the Year WA Point Score 1994. He also has numerous Best in Group awards. Rhubarb is now about to enjoy a show career in Singapore for about 12 months with Teresa and Ben Chia.

Tarawera Jeune is bred by Miss Wren and owned by Mrs Hingeley. She is a very sound bitch, of excellent dark blue colour and tan, with a lovely feminine head and expression. She is a very true-moving bitch coming and going. She started her show career at 12 months of age, and now, at just 20 months, is already halfway to her Championship title. A class in Group winner and Best in Show, ASTC of WA Open Show, she has a bright show career ahead of her. Aust. Fin. Ch. Karlyermai Cool Dude is bred and owned by Mrs S. Baxter and is a Runner Up in Show, Class in Show, Runner Up in Group and Class in Group winner. He is competing successfully at both Specialty and All Breeds Shows, in several States of Australia under local, interstate and international Judges. Dude was the Top Winning Australian Silky Terrier of the Year WA Point Score 1995, winning this award at the age of two and a half years. He travelled to Europe in late 1995 and has successfully completed his Finnish Championship title. He is now well on his way to his International Titles with CACIBs awarded in several countries, plus Exhibit in Group and Group placings to his credit. His European campaign is in the capable hands of M. Krstic (Croatia) and S. Vallimaa-Koskimaa (Finland).

THE SILKY IN NEW ZEALAND

The first Silky was registered in New Zealand in 1909. Her name was Fluff and she whelped to Cadger and Judy and bred by a Mrs Druckwater. This was at the time when they were known as 'Sydney Silkies'. In those days it was not necessary to have complete information about a dog in order to register it, which makes it virtually impossible now to trace the origins of these early dogs. Nowadays, a dog must have a four-generation pedigree before being registered in New Zealand. In 1915 a dog called Silver Prince was registered, who was whelped in 1911 to Silver King and Snips. Silver Prince, and a bitch named Silver Queen, were to become New Zealand's first Champion Australian Silky Terriers. The first recorded import from Australia was Sir Roger of Tibet, who came from Templestowe in Victoria. He was born on May 30th 1947 and registered in New Zealand on July 19th 1947. In the late 1960s the late Mrs Guinibert imported Ch. Tamworth Victoria and Ch. Tamworth Blue Aussie from Victoria, Australia. These two specimens were a beautiful blue and tan. The late Mrs Robb imported Lylac Smithy from New South Wales, Australia.

The New Zealand show standard is comparable to that in Australia. To become a Champion, a dog must be awarded eight challenge certificates, one of these must be won after the age of 12 months. Puppies must be four months old before they can be shown. Classes are as follows: Baby Puppy, four to six months; Puppy, six to twelve months; Junior, one to two years; Intermediate, two to three years; NZ Bred,

Aust. N.Z. Ch. Tarawera Rag A Muffen (Aust. Ch. Valanne Sir Richard – Aust. Ch. Tarawera Kimlanne).

any age; Open, any age. Dogs are able to be awarded a challenge certificate after six months of age. In the past it was not unusual to have up to twenty dogs at shows. Unfortunately, now the average would be between four and ten. Although Silkies are very popular pets, most people choose not to show their dogs for various reasons.

Although small in numbers many of the breed have made their presence felt on the show circuit. The first Silky to win an All Breeds Best in Show was Aust. NZ Ch. Dulcannina Robbie. He was imported from Australia. Another Silky was Aust. NZ Ch. Tarawera Rag A Muffen, who took the second Best in Show award. Robyn Campbell's NZ Ch. Premium of Winapisarki also won a Best in Show during his illustrious show career. Aust. Ch. Tarawera Coolhand Luke, Aust. NZ Ch. Tarawera My Steel Dan, Aust. NZ Ch. Kamaroon of Kelbrae and NZ Ch. Premonition of Altmark have all had Reserve Best in Show at All Breeds in New Zealand.

From the 1970s onwards there have been many Australian dogs imported into New Zealand. A good proportion of these have come from the Tarawera Kennels; there are not too many pedigrees that do not have a Tarawera prefix somewhere in their bloodline. Some have stayed, others have obtained their NZ title and returned to Australia to obtain a dual title. Among other well-known Australian kennels to export dogs to New Zealand were: Dulcannina (Mrs F. Camac); Valanne (the late Mrs A. Richardson); Adamanda (Miss R. Bennett); Guruga (the late Mrs J. Walker); Rydale (Mr and Mrs E. Watt) and Penannji (Mr J. Skippen) to name a few. New Zealand has also exported several Silkies that have stamped their mark around the world: Jean and Ray McKay's NZ-born Aust. NZ Ch. Bams Boy of Lakemba; Colleen and Grahame Mold's NZ-bred Aust. Ch. Mahald Shilo Blue, and, from Anne Crenfeldt's kennel Kelbrae, comes Aust. Singapore Ch. Hijack of Kelbrae, Aust. Ch. Kelbrae Rhubarb, and last but not least Aust. NZ Ch. Kamaroon of Kelbrae – the most successful Silky ever bred in New Zealand.

12 THE SILKY TERRIER IN BRITAIN

A guide to the number of Silkies in Britain is obtained by looking at the registrations of Australian Silky Terriers with the Kennel Club from 1984 to 1994. 37 were registered in 1984, 69 in 1985, 31 in 1986, 56 in 1987, 25 in 1988, 39 in 1989, 54 in 1990, 46 in 1991, 42 in 1992, 11 in 1993 and 15 in 1994. In the early 1980s Silkies were being exhibited in Crufts in the Not Separately Classified classes, together with Border Collies and many other breeds without their own classes. It was not until 1987 that all breeds acknowledged by the Kennel Club were given classes, and in that year Dorpentune Bobby Shaftoe won Best Dog and BOB, with his litter sister Dorpentune Blue Lilac at Hidalgo making Best Bitch. In 1988 the Best Dog was Lenbar Blue boy, bred and owned by Len and Barbara Lee. Best Bitch and BOB was Jardin de Fleur, bred and owned by Mr and Mrs Lumbus. In 1989 and 1990 Best Dog and BOB was Bragan Jolly Swagman. Best Bitch was Dorpentune Blue Lilac at Hidalgo, both owned by Mrs M. Semple. In 1991 Best Dog and BOB when to Bragan Call Me Sydney, bred by Mollie Semple and owned by Mr and Mrs Saxby. The Best Bitch was Marshdae Kiah

who was bred and owned by Anne Marshall. Bragan Call Me Sydney triumphed again in 1992, while the Best Bitch was Marshdae Mattilda of Silandigeorg who Anne Marshall bred and who is owned by Mr and Mrs Nevett. In 1993 the Nevetts Silandigeorg Boomerang, who they had also bred, went Best Dog, and Best Bitch and BOB was Marshdae Taaronga of Martre, bred by Anne Marshall and owned by Mr and Mrs Roberts. In 1994 the Best Dog and BOB was Sharhad Kempsey at Chatcombe, bred by Mr and Mrs Sharp and owned by Mrs Graham. The Best Bitch was Sharhad Sweet n Sharp, bred and owned by the Sharps. In 1995 the Best Dog was again Bragan Call Me Sydney, and the Best Bitch and BOB was again Sharhad Sweet n Sharp. Bobby Shaftoe is still the only Silky to win Best In Show at Championship level, which he did at the UK Toydog Championship show in 1993.

SILKY BREEDERS IN BRITAIN

The Australian Silky Terrier has not yet, fortunately, become a popular pet dog with the general public. The feeling among breeders is that this is fortunate, because they did not want to see this superb breed spoiled beyond recognition due to overbreeding. Silky owners and breeders did not wish to compete with the popularity of the Yorkshire Terrier as a house dog and family pet. When out walking with a Silky, people still mistake the dog for a Yorkshire. It is not until the main differences are pointed out to them that they see they were wrong. The UK has no large Australian Silky kennels, but it does have a number of small establishments who have concentrated on the breed. The main Australian influences on British Silkies came from Dulcannina, Lylac, Glenpetite, Milan and Kaylaw. It is from these few lines that they have developed the Silky as it is now in Britain. These are a few of the Australian Silky affix holders in Britain.

Apico Blue Mist of Marshdae, pictured at six months of age.

APICO

This affix belongs to Don Garbett (and his late wife Barbara) –although it is no longer active in the breed. The principal dog from them was Apico Dutchboy. He was one of the first to be seen in the British show ring. His pet name was Boy, and he was shown by Barbara. His breeding was from Connalee, Kaylaw and Penannji lines. Apico Glenpetite Lolita was one of their bitches, shown only a little. Her breeding was from Milan and Tamworth lines and she was imported into Britain by Don and Barbara. She had only a short life due to a fatal accident.

It was from a mating of Boy and Lolita that Anne Marshall obtained Apico Blue Mist in 1981. Duskhunter Dolly of Apico was their second bitch. Her breeding was influenced by Swedish lines – Vasterbackens, Augusta and Lillgardens, to name just a few. Wybilena Wirana at Apico started his show life with Barbara but later

went down to Barbara and Len Lee, who were relatively new in Silkies at that time. Unfortunately Barbara's health deteriorated, so they moved to the warmer climate of Malaga in Spain, taking with them Boy and Dulcannina Cassandra. Barbara still wanted to show the dogs, which she did, making them both up to International Champions. They also increased their kennel in Spain, breeding many more Silkies which unfortunately were left there. Time caught up with Barbara. She died in 1994. Don eventually returned to England but has retired from active work with the Silky.

BRAGAN

When Mollie Semple visited Australia some years ago, she took with her a task to perform for a friend – she had to look up some Australian Silkies. Her assignment was to collect as much information and photographs of the "real thing" as possible.

RIGHT:
Bragan Jolly
Swagman: Bred
and owned by
Molly Semple.

BELOW:
Bragan Call Me
Sydney.

Mollie searched for these dogs, which she had never seen, and when she first saw the Silky on home ground she was not impressed. However, she did as she was asked, and took photographs. She even attended a seminar in order to learn a little more about these "scruffy little things", as she described them. Little did she know that, before long, she would be owning not one, but two "scruffy little things".

Her first Austraian Silky was a bitch from the Dorpentune litter born in quarantine, namely Dorpentune Blue Lilac. Mollie showed her at all levels, and believe me, she was presented to perfection. She won many awards including Best Bitch at Crufts the year her litter brother, Bobby Shaftoe, took Best of Breed. Blue went on to win many BOBs or Best of Sex at Championship level and at the AST Society's shows. She was mated to Marshdae Koobor of Gerallyn. From this litter came Bragan Jolly Swagman. He was BOB at Crufts in 1989 and 1990, owned and shown by Mollie. When she mated son back to mother, this produced the most consistent winning Silky, Bragan Call Me Sydney, owned by Mr and Mrs A. Saxby, shown by Sonia Saxby. Syd is Sonia's one and only Silky. He lives together with Sonia's Min Pins and Border Collies. Sonia only keeps male dogs and they get on fine together.

DERLAN

Alan and Kath Larder registered the Derlan affix which was used first on American Cocker Spaniels, a breed they both loved and which was very successful. Their first Silky was Dorpentune Bobby Shaftoe. Both Kath and Alan were well-known for their presentation. Bobby was presented just perfectly. The Larders had developed this art from years of grooming American

Marshdae Tumbaarumba at Derlan: Exported to Sweden where he became an International Champion, and Top Dog 1995.
Photo: Trafford.

Cocker Spaniels for the show ring. Their greatest win with Bobby must have been taking the top spot at the 1983 United Kingdom Toydog Society when he went Best in Show. Bobby was a firm favourite with them both, but Alan took charge on most occasions. Together they won BOB at Crufts the first year that classes were scheduled. When it was time for Bobby to retire, they turned to me for a youngster. This was Marshdae Tumbaarumba at Derlan who was show-trained by Alan, taking many top spots before being exported to Sweden where he quickly settled in to a different routine. He soon gained his International Championship title and was Top Dog in Sweden 1995.

DUSKHUNTER

This affix belongs to Miss Linda Stewart who owned Glenpetite Wata Boy (imported from Australia) and a bitch from Ireland,

Coolmine Boobah. Linda only showed Wata Boy for a short time, concentrating on producing a few puppies, some of which were seen in the show ring.

HIDALGO

Two bitches from the Dorpentune litter carry this affix, Dorpentune Lilac time, owned by Mrs Val Marsden, and Hidalgo Blue Lilac owned by Mollie Semple. They are litter sisters to Bobby Shaftoe. Val showed Lilac Time for only a short while, though many people thought her to be better than Blue Lilac. Val's affix Hidalgo is seen through the Chihuahua pedigrees.

LENBAR

Barbara and Len Lee's first Silky, Sholeen The Swagman, came from Eileen Spavin. He was the first of many to be shown by them. Their first bitch was Apico Blue Susan, a litter sister to M Blue Mist. Len and Barbara stayed loyal members of the Society from the very beginning. Unfortunately they both suffered health problems and could not continue showing their dogs. They stayed with the Society, attending functions whenever they could; even over the last 12 months they still kept an interest in the goings-on of the Silky. Barbara died early in 1996 with Len following her in the June of that same year.

Dorpentune Blue Lilac at Hidalgo.

Marshdae Minkilliko at Chomedey. Owned and photographed by Mark Burns.

MARSHDAE

Anne Marshall's introduction to this delightful breed came in 1979 with, as has been mentioned earlier, her meeting with a young male puppy – and they fell for each other at once. Carol Bacon, who was active in those days in the Papillon circle, had suggested they visited Manchester to see some puppies. Anne had thought they were going to see a litter of Papillons. Instead they saw Silkies, and Apico Archie travelled on her knee the whole way home. He converted her and she says she will never be without this breed, they are something so special. His long and active life ended at almost 17 years of age on May 1st 1996. He died in his sleep, never having suffered a day's illness in his life.

Aussie was very successful in the early days in the Not Separately Classified classes at all levels of shows. Indeed there were very few breed classes anywhere in the early eighties. A male puppy from a mating of Aussie to Wybilena Kaarimba of Marshdae, Marshdae Koobor of Gerallyn, owned by Alan and Geraldine Tomlinson did well in the breed. He also sired some very nice puppies. It was Wybilena Kaarimba (pet name Kaari), that instigated Anne's use of Aboriginal and Australian names for her puppies. The Kennel Club actually contacted her following an application to register a litter, asking where her unusual names and their spellings came from.

Probably one of her most successful litters was one where Anne mated Mist (Apico Blue Mist at Marshdae) to Dorpentune Bobby Shaftoe, owned by Alan and Kath Larder. From this litter, which was whelped on June 22nd 1983

139

Balkana Whata Time at Marshdae (imp.). Photo: Russell Fine Art.

and contained two males and four females, came M. Mamunna, whom she kept. Munna had four litters, each one containing six puppies, the majority of them being bitches. She went on to win Top Brood Bitch year after year. Also in that litter Anne had M. Maldanna, a dog with a wonderful coat. It took a long time to grow – in fact at eight months she almost sold him because his coat length was still only a couple of inches long. He won at all levels, including Best in Show at one of the AST Society shows under Percy Whittaker.

Anne had to seek Kennel Club approval to mate Munna. She was nearing her eighth birthday when the Kennel Club introduced a new ruling "that the Kennel Club would not register puppies born to a bitch who was eight and over". Anne's intention was to mate her to Paddy (Balkana Whata Time at Marshdae), whom she had imported from Australia, and who had not yet been released from quarantine – hence her appeal, which she won. Nine weeks later there arrived four females and two males: this was now Anne's "Whata" litter.

SHARHAD

In 1986 Mr and Mrs D. Sharp purchased a bitch puppy from Gladys McKenna, Tarbockgreen Blue Saphire (Marshdae Maldanna ex Dekobras Blue Lace at Tarbockgreen) and, as with so many before her, June Sharp was bitten by the Silky bug. June has worked hard with her Silkies. She has hit the top spot with Sharhad Sweet n Sharp (Bragan Jolley Swagman ex Tarbockgreen Blue Saphire at Sharhad). This bitch has been very successful in the show ring.

Other affixes being carried by Silkies are Dekobras, Pomeroywoods, Sholeen, Northrise, Tarbockgreen, Silandigeorge, Martre and Merebeck. Unfortunately not all of these affixes are active today.

13 THE SILKY TERRIER IN NORTH AMERICA

In this chapter you will read about a number of class wins and awards and titles you may not be familiar with, so I will take a moment to enlighten you (*writes* **Donna Renton**).

ROM – Award of Merit, Top Producer. Sires must produce ten Champion get to receive this title and dams must produce a total of four.

ROMX – Award of Merit, Top Producer-Excellent. Sires must produce twenty Champion get and dams must produce eight.

Weeblu's Blaze of Joy Memorial Award. This Award is offered to the owner-handler of the Silky which has defeated the greatest number of Silkies in the breed for the entire calendar year.

Iradell Trophy. This trophy is awarded to the Silky with the most Best of Breed wins during the calendar year where there are points in the classes when at least two owners have Silkies in competition.

Awards of Merit. These are awarded to Silkies which the Specialty Judge feels are 'almost' of equal quality to the Best of Breed winner. They are awarded to no more than ten per cent of the Silkies remaining in the ring after the Best of Breed has been judged.

National Specialty shows. Each year one National Specialty Show is held in the US.

Sweepstakes. Only non-Champion Silkies from 6 to 18 months of age are eligible to enter. Classes are: 6 to 9 months puppy, male and female; 9 to 12 months puppy, male and female; 12 to 15 months dog and bitch classes; and 15 to 18 months dog and bitch classes. All dog and bitch classes are judged separately. All class winners go on to compete for best in Sweepstakes and Best Opposite Sex in Sweepstakes. There are no Championship points awarded for Sweepstakes wins and licensed judges do not judge in Sweeps. (Judges are usually chosen from people working toward obtaining their Silky licence.)

In the regular classes any Silky aged 6 months or older is eligible to enter. Classes are: 6 to 9 months puppy dog and bitch; 9 to 12 months puppy dog and bitch; novice dog and bitch; American-bred dog and bitch; bred-by-exhibitor dog and bitch; 12 to 18 months dog and bitch; and Open dog and bitch. Dog and bitch classes are judged separately. All males winning a class compete for Winners Dog and all females winning their class compete for Winners Bitch. From these two winners, a Best of Winners is chosen. All Champions entered in Best of Breed, as well as the veteran dog and bitch class winners, and Winners Dog and Winners Bitch, compete for Best of Breed and Best of Opposite Sex. All puppy class winners compete for Best Puppy in Specialty Show. Specialty wins are highly prized because of the overall quality of the competition at these shows, as well as the large numbers entered. Sweepstakes entries average between 80 and 100 Silkies, and Regular class entries average between 175 and 200 Silkies.

LEADING US BREEDERS AND LINES

MONET
CATRINA MARTIN
Vancouver, Washington.
In 1983 Catrina Martin obtained her first Silky from long-time breeder Janet Mathews of Sonnyvale Silkies. She bred her bitch, Sonnyvale Kachina Hope, known as Penny, in 1985, to Ch. Kiku's Safire Sgt. Brodie. From this breeding came Catrina's foundation bitch, Monet's Merrie Sunshine, known as Sunny. Sunny was never shown, because Catrina was a student at that time. In due course Sunny produced five Champions and was awarded her Register of Merit, Top Producer title (ROM). One of Sunny's get, Ch. Monet's Just a Bit of Jazz, was Winners Dog and Best of Winners at the 1991 Silky Terrier Club of America National Specialty. His sire is Ch. Amron's O'Bear Shariff.

Sunny's daughter, Ch. Amron's Monet's Bear, is the dam of Ch. Amron's T.J. Bear Extraordinaire, who is currently living and being successfully shown in the UK. Sunny

Am. Ch. Monet's Luck Be A Lady: Group winning Silky, Number One US Silky female for 1996.   Photo: Bernard Kernan.

is also the grandmother of Am. Can. Ch. Monet's Luck Be a Lady, 'Lucky', who was the number one Silky female in the US in 1995. Lucky is also a Group winning Silky. Lucky is sired by Ch. Amron's Reebok A Blue Bear and is out of Ch. Monet's Ain't Misbehavin. Catrina Martin breeds on a limited basis, incorporating careful thought and planning into her breeding program. She has future plans to produce litters sired by Am. Can. Ch. Lucknow Local Talent, ROM, and Am. Can. Int. Ch. Tawny Mist Copyright. She names all her Silkies after musical themes because of her middle name and kennel name, Monet, and because she has always loved music and is currently singing soprano with the Portland Philharmonic Choir.

TAWNY MIST
STEPHEN AND DONNA RENTON
Beavercreek, Oregon.
The Rentons obtained their first Silky, Ch. Tara Lara Travlin Man, in 1982. They became interested in showing and contacted a local exhibitor, Lee Easton-Bergum (Easton's Silkies), who helped them find their way into the show ring. She acted as friend and mentor and taught them what they needed to know to become successful exhibitors.

A few years later they obtained Ch. Tiffanees Top Drawer Sapphire and Ch. Lucknow Crystal Image. In due course, Sapphire obtained her Championship and went on to produce five Champions, giving her the title of Top Producer, ROM. One of Sapphire's daughters, Ch. Tawny Mist Touch of Class, ROMX, has had a positive impact on the breed. Classy produced a total of 11 Champions, eight of which were top in the National Specials and/or Group winners and/or Group placers. Classy is the daughter of Ch. Weeblu's Trailblazer of Don-El, ROMX. Trailblazer has an impressive show record and was, at one time, the top winning Silky in the US. He is also a multiple all-breed Best in Show winner and multiple Specialty Best in Show winner. He is also the sire of many fine Silkies. Classy is Trail's only ROMX daughter. Classy was bred back to her father and produced Am. Can. Ch. Tawny

Am. Ch. Tawny Mist Classic Blueprint ROM (Am. Ch. Weeblu's Trailblazer of Don-El – Am. Ch. Tawny Mist Touch of Class ROMX).   Photo courtesy: Donna Renton.

Mist Classical Blues, 'Rocky', and Ch. Tawny Mist Classic Blueprint, ROM, known as Rambo. Rambo and Rocky were both top US Specials in 1989. Rocky is owned by Debbie and Nona Nelson, of Hopepark Silkies, from Canada. He is a top producer in Canada as well as a US Group winner and Group placer in both the US and Canada. Rambo still lives with the Rentons and is still an active stud. To date

Am. Ch. Tawny Mist Touch of Class ROMX (Am. Ch. Weeblu's Trailblazer of Don-El – Am. Ch. Tiffanees Top Drawer Sapphire ROM): Foundation for Tawny Mist Silkys.

Photo: Steven Ross.

Am. Ch. Tawny Mist Crystal Gale ROMX: Best of Opposite in Sweepstakes and Best Puppy at the 1989 National Specialty.

he has produced 17 Champions, many of which are Group winners and/or placers. He is the sire of Ch. Tawny Mist Crystal Gale, ROMX, Ch. Tawny Mist Crystal Chrisma, and Ch. Tawny Mist Amron Rona Bearit, who is referred to later in this chapter. Classy was also bred to a renowned stud, Ch. Marina's Houston, ROMX. She produced a litter of two females, Ch. Tawny Mist Touch of Spice and Am. Int. Ch. Tawny Mist Touch of Excitement, both of which easily obtained their Championships. Touch of Excitement, known as Erica, was a top US Special in 1994 and is a multiple Group placing Silky.

The Rentons obtained Lucknow Crystal Image, 'Crissy', from Stephanie Monteleone in 1984. Crissy easily obtained her Championship and was Winners Bitch and Best of Winners at the 1985 National Specialty. She is the dam of eight Champions and obtained her ROMX title as a result. One of Crissy's daughters, Ch. Tawny Mist Crystal Gale, ROMX, was Best Opposite Sex in Sweepstakes and Best Puppy in Specialty Show at the 1989 National Specialty. Gale also left her mark as a top producer-excellent, producing nine Champions. Her son, Am. Can. Int. Ch. Tawny Mist Crystal Chrisma, was a top in the National Specialty in 1993 and 1994. He is a multiple Group placing Silky and is also a Group winner. Crissy's son, Am. IABKC, Int. Fr. Ch. Tawny Mist Crystal

Tawny Mist Best Kept Secret: Group 1st, Alpo National Grand Championship, Best Puppy in Specialty show, 1996.

Ashbey Photography.

Terminator lives in Paris, France, with François Estas. Prior to leaving for France, Terminator produced a number of nice Silkies, including Ch. Tawny Mist Trade Mark, a multiple Group winning and Group placing Silky, and Ch. Amron's T.J. Bear Extraordinaire.

Ch. Tawny Mist Trade Mark, and his son, Ch. Tawny Mist Copyright, were both top US Specials in 1995. On the way to his Championship, Cory was Best Puppy in Specialty Show at the 1993 National Specialty. He finished his US title by the time he was 10 months old by taking wins over the adults on numerous occasions. He is a multiple Group winning Silky in both the US and Canada. He was the Pedigree Award winner and Iradell Award winner, defeating more Silkies nationwide than any other Silky in the US during 1995. He is currently the number one US Silky for 1996. Cory is owned by the Rentons, Ralph Owen from Spokane, Wa., and Dorothy Hicks from Cypress, Ca. Cory's niece, Tawny Mist Best Kept Secret, was Best Puppy in Specialty Show and Reserve Winners Bitch at the 1996 National Specialty. She is also a puppy Group winner and has taken Championship points over adult competition. She is co-owned by Irma Marshall and Donna Renton.

In 1994 the Rentons purchased an addition to their breeding program, Ch. Marina's Tawny Mist C Quest. Known as Luke, he was sired by Ch. Lucknow Local Talent, ROM, and is out of Ch. Easton's Esprit, ROM. Luke is co-owned by Donna Renton and Carol Dunster of Washtucna, Wa. Luke is the sire of some excellent quality puppies, including Tawny Mist Best Kept Secret and Tawny Mist Cool Silk, who was Best Opposite Sex in Sweepstakes at the 1996 National Specialty. The Rentons believe a sound mind and body are both essential for a Silky. They take pride in striving to produce the best quality Silkies they can. When they breed they use a combination of line breeding, outcrossing and, occasionally, in-breeding. They are always careful to avoid breeding problems into the breed. Having set a high standard for themselves, they have been successful as breeders and have produced more than 70 Champions since 1982.

CENTARRA
Pam and Paul Laperruque
Romona, California

The Laperruques have been involved in Silkies for more than 20 years. Pam became interested in them when her boss's wife placed a cute cuddly Silky puppy in her arms – it was love at first sight. Their most cherished stud, Tak'ope Tu Shu, ROMX, found his way to the Laperruques after he had been passed from pillar to post. During his travels he had, sadly, developed a mistrust of people. After he came to live with Pam and Paul, even though he was of excellent quality, they decided they did not want to put Tu Shu through the stress of the show ring. As far as they were concerned, he didn't need to prove himself in the ring. However, he definitely proved what he was made of by producing 48 Champions, many of which have excelled in the show ring.

One of his sons, Ch. Centarra's Trivial Pursuit, 'Trevor', is the winner of three consecutive Best in Specialty Show breed wins at the Coast regional Specialty. He was the number one US Silky during 1987, 1988 and 1989, and was also the Iradell trophy winner for those years. Trevor has also won the Weeblu's Blaze of Joy Award and received multiple Awards of Merit at National Specialties. He is a multiple Group winner and Group placer. Trevor has a total of 16 Champion get to date. Another of Tu Shu's sons, Ch. Houzabout Pal Joey, was Winners Dog and Best of Winners at the 1991 Coast Specialty. He went on to be a top US Silky with multiple Group placings. Tu Shu's daughter, Ch. Carousel's Jingle Bell Shus was Best of

Tak 'Ope Tu Shu ROMX:
Sire of 48 Champions.

Am. Ch. Centarra's Trivial Pursuit: Group winning Silky, Iradell and Blaze of Joy award winner.

Photo: Missy Yuhl.

Opposite Sex at three consecutive Coast Specialties for 1989, 1990 and 1991. The Laperruques are still breeding Silkies, but only on a limited basis. Over the years Pam has become an expert toy breed handler, which keeps her very busy. They have made major contributions to the breed and plan to continue to do so in the future.

AMRON
NORMA AND TOM BAUGH
Cypress, Texas.

The Baughs have been breeding and showing dogs for many years. They started with Yorkshire Terriers, added English Springers for Tom, then branched out into Lakeland Terriers, Australian Terriers and Silkies, which they became active with in 1980. Their daughter, Schelle, came up with the Amron Kennel prefix by spelling Norma backwards. Their first breeding produced Ch. Amron Crystal Pistol, who became their foundation brood bitch. Crystal was bred to top producer Ch. Marina's Dallas and that combination produced their foundation studs, Ch. Amron's Hug a Bear, ROMX, and Ch. Amron's I Don't Care Bear, ROM. Huggy has produced 33 Champions to date but, at age twelve, he is no longer standing at stud. Huggy is behind almost all of the Amron Champions. The Baughs breeding philosophy is primarily based on line breeding and careful selection.

Huggy is the sire of some excellent Silkies, among which is Ch. Amron's Sensasha Bear, known as Cindy. Cindy was the number one Silky in the US in 1989 and 1990. She was always owner-handled by Norma during that time. Cindy's litter-mate, Dorrie, Ch. Amron's Adora-Bear, was the number one Silky in Canada during that same period, and is a Canadian Best in Show winner. The Baughs also produced a US National Specialty Best in Show winner and Canadian Best in Show winner, Am. Can. Ch. Amron Silver Sassafras. In 1994 Norma won the title for Top Winning Silky Terrier, Owner-Handled, with Ch. Tawny Mist Amron Rona Bearit. Rona was also the number one US Silky Female that year and is a Group winner and multiple Group placer. Norma and her Silkies have won owner-handler awards for a number of years.

In September 1995 the Baughs exported a Silky male to England, Ch. Amron's T.J. Bear Extraordinaire. He is now co-owned by Norma and June Sharp from England. T.J. lives with June in Birmingham. He is, as I mentioned earlier, the product of the Amron and Tawny Mist lines, his dam being Ch. Amron's Monet Bear and his sire is Ch. Tawny Mist Crystal Terminator, now

Am. Ch. Amron's Hug-A-Bear ROMX (Am. Ch. Marina's Dallas – Am. Ch. Amron's Crystal Pistol): Sire of 33 US Champions.

Am. Ch. Amron's Sensasha Bear II – sired by Am. Ch. Amron's Hug-A-Bear ROMX – Number One Silky Terrier in 1989 and 1990.

owned by François Estas and living in France. He was exported there shortly after T.J. was born. Two weeks after T.J. ended his 6 month quarantine he was in the show ring, taking Best of Breed from the miscellaneous classes, and he went on to a Toy Group First. A couple of weeks later he won Best in Show at a Silky Terrier Specialty in England.

The Baughs take pride in producing quality Silkies. They also enjoy starting new exhibitors in the breed. During their time in Silkies they have produced more than 70 Champions. Having bred both Yorkshire Terriers and Australian Terriers, they feel Silkies are the best of both breeds, being sturdier built than the Yorkie while retaining the glamour of the long silky coat

Am. Ch. Tawny Mist Amron Rona Bearit (Am. Ch. Tawny Mist Classic Blueprint – Am. Ch. Amron Tawny Mist Gypsie Bear): 1994 Number One US Silky female and Number One owner-handled Silky. Handled exclusively by Norma Baugh.
Photo: Bernard Kernan.

and, of course, retaining the wonderful outgoing terrier temperament. To date the Baughs continue to produce show pups and offer stud services. They are very active in showing and are involved with the Gulf Coast Silky Terrier Club.

LUCKNOW
WILLIAM AND STEPHANY MONTELEONE
New Orleans, Louisiana

Stephany purchased her first Silky for her sister, which she showed and finished in 1981. Stephany enjoyed the Silky so much that she and her husband, William, decided they needed one of their own. They obtained their Silky from Verna Tucker of Fawn Hill Silky Terriers. Their foundation

bitch was Ch. Fawn Hill Lucknow Lead-N-Lady. They called her Mrs Bridget. Mrs Bridget was very special to the Monteleones and set their future in Silkies. She finished her Championship easily and was Winners Bitch and Best of Winners at a National Specialty along the way. She produced some nice puppies, among which were Ch. Lucknow Crystal Image and Ch. Lucknow Center Stage. Crystal Image was Winners Bitch and Best of Winners at the 1985 National Specialty and is owned by Steve and Donna Renton. Her sister, Center Stage, went on to be a top Special. Mrs Bridget ultimately became a ROM.

The Monteleones purchased another Silky from Verna Tucker, Ch. Fawn Hill Lucknow Sweet 'n' Sour, called Jennifer. Stephany exhibited Jennifer to a remarkable show career. Jennifer took many Group wins and placements. She won two all-breed Bests in Show and had three consecutive Best in Specialty Show wins, retiring with the Wexford Pogo three-time Challenge Trophy. She finished her show career by becoming the top winning Silky Terrier female in US history. Jennifer then went on to make history as a mother. Out of four litters, she produced eight Champions, giving her the title of ROMX. In her last litter of four males, she produced three American Champions. They were sired by Ch. Marina's Houston, ROMX. One male, Ch. Lucknow Liquid Asset, is owned by Mr and Mrs Hartmann, who reside in Holland. He has an impressive international show record and is a German Best in Show winner. The second male, Ch. Lucknow Legal Counsel, is owned by François Estas in France. Like his brother, he made an impression on the international show scene as a Best in Show winner.

149

Am. Ch. Fawn Hill Lucknow Sweet n' Sour: Top winning Silky female in US history, winner of two all-breed Best in Show and three consecutive National Specialty Best of Breed wins.

The Monteleones kept the third male, Am. Can. Ch. Lucknow Local Talent, who continued the Lucknow tradition. They called this special Silky CC Rider. CC definitely followed in his dam's paw prints. He was shown by Barbara Heckerman to 10 All Breed Best in Show wins, over 50 Group firsts, and numerous Group placements. CC's remarkable record makes him the Top Winning Silky Terrier in US history. Not only has CC proven his quality in the show ring but he has gone on to make his mark as a producer. He is currently seven years old and has already obtained his ROM title. He also holds the distinction of being the only Silky in US history to produce the Best of Breed, Best of Opposite Sex, Winners Dog and Best of Winners/Best in Sweepstakes at one National Specialty. These 1996 National Specialty Winners are: Best of Breed, Ch. Derringdew Lucknow Winston, owned by Mr John P. Scheidt and Donald M. Spear; Best of Opposite Sex, Ch. Snowsilk's Jazz

Dancer, owned by Judy Carson and Bernadette Fletcher. Best in Sweepstakes, Winners Dog and Best of Winners, went to Anova's Prime Time who is owned and shown by his breeders, Michael and Suellen Shanker. CC has also produced two US All Breed Best in Show and Best in Specialty Show winners, Ch. Derringdew Lucknow Winston and Ch. Marina's C Monster. The Monteleones breed on a very limited basis and do not usually have pups available, however CC continues to stand at stud to approved bitches. I believe Stephany has looked into the possibilty of a frozen semen bank for CC so he can continue to make his mark on the breed long into the future.

LAPSITTER
DIANE MAGNUSON
Salisbury CT
Diane Magnuson started in Silkies in 1975 under the kennel name of Lapsitter. She continued a successful breeding program from that time and didn't begin breeding with Bernadette Fletcher and Judy Carson until quite a bit later. Diane's foundation bitch, Ch. Royaline Lapsitters Peach Jam, ROM, was a beautiful show bitch with multiple Group placings, and was quite a producer. Her foundation stud was Ch. Kiku's Kilee's Blue Denim, known as Wrangler. From these Silkies came Ch. Lapsitter's Blue Denim Rags, ROM, who was also a multiple Group placer. Wrangler was also the sire of Ch. Lakewind Skip Jack, who is a dog of excellent soundness and type, and Ch. Lapsitters Pennyblue Spark, 'Sparkle', whom Diane sold to Bernadetter Fletcher on a co-ownership. They then performed a half-brother half-sister breeding that produced Ch. Glen Row Lapsitter's Crystal, ROM.

Am. Ch. Glen Row Lapsitters Crystal: Multiple Group-placing Silky.
Photo: Chuck Tatham.

Am. Ch. Lapsitters Marina's Wild Thyme: Multiple Group-placing Silky and Award of Merit 1990 National Specialty.
Ashbey Photography.

Am. Can. Ch. Lakewind Skip Jack.

Am. Ch. Glen Row Lapsitters Cartier: Best in Sweepstakes winner, 1995 National Specialty.   Photo: Callea.

Crystal had a nice show career with multiple Group placings, Best of Breed at the prestigious Westminster Kennel Club and Award of Merit at the 1990 National Specialty. She also proved to be an excellent producer. Out of three litters she produced seven Champions. Her first breeding was to Ch. Lucknow Local Talent, ROM, which produced an all-Champion litter of four, one of which is Ch. Snowsilk's Jazz Dancer. Dancer is co-owned by Bernadette Fletcher and Judy Carson. She was Award of Merit and Best Opposite Sex at the 1993 and 1996 National Specialties. Her litter sister, Ch. Glen-Row's All That Jazz, was Best Puppy in Specialty Show during 1992.

Crystal's next breeding was to Ch. Weeblu's Trailblazer of Don-El, ROMX, which produced two Champions. For her third breeding, Crystal was in-bred to her half-brother, Ch. Marina's Wild Thyme, known as Sizzle. Ch. Glen Row Lapsitters

Cartier is the result of this breeding. Cartier was Best in Sweepstakes, Winners Bitch, Best Opposite Sex and Award of Merit at the 1995 National Specialty. During 1996 she was Best of Breed at Westminster and she recently won a Group First. Cartier's sire, Sizzle, presented himself nicely in the show ring. Diane Magnuson feels he very closely resembles her ideal Silky in color, head and overall type. He was Award of Merit at the 1994 National Specialty and is a Group winning and multiple Group placing Silky.

Diane Magnuson only breeds in an attempt to improve the quality of the Silky Terrier. Some tips for a successful breeding program include knowing as much as you can about all the dogs in a five-generation pedigree, and studying your pedigree while determining what you wish to accomplish. Try to go to as many Specialties as you possibly can to view other Silkies and, lastly, don't be in a big hurry to sell your pups. Give them time to mature for color, coat texture and size.

UP AND COMING BREEDERS

SHALEE
SHAUNA LEE JONES
Oklahoma City, Oklahoma
Shauna obtained her first Silky for show in 1987. She quickly became interested in becoming a Silky breeder. She learned a lot about breeding and showing with the encouragement of Ivy Rogers (Jenini Silkies) and Louise Bialek (Dunar Silkies), both from California. Shauna's foundation Silkies came from the Dunar and Jenini lines. Ivy acted as Shauna's mentor and introduced her to the wonderful world of showing dogs. Louise coached and drilled into Shauna the importance of sound

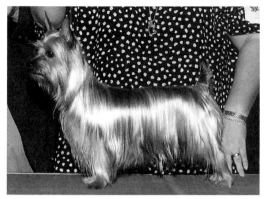

Am. Ch. Tawny Mist Once Bitten ROM:
Dam of Am. Ch. Tawny Mist Shalee Del Rio
and Am. Ch. Shalee Tawny Mist Royal Silk.

Am. Ch. Tawny Mist Shalee Royal Silk (Am.
Ch. Marina's Tawny Mist C Quest – Am.
Ch. Tawny Mist Once Bitten ROM).
Photo: Petrulis.

structure in a breeding program. After Shauna moved to Oklahoma she continued breeding and showing. She has been quite successful in the midwest. Shauna expanded her foundation Silkies by obtaining Ch. Tawny Mist Once Bitten, who she co-owned with her breeder, Donna Renton. The combined breeding of Shalee and Tawny Mist has produced some fine Silkies, such as Am. Can. Ch. Tawny Mist Shalee Galveston, called Gage, Ch. Tawny Mist Shalee Del Rio, Ch. Shalee Tawny Mist Royal Silk, 'Roy', and Ch. Tawny Mist Shalee Bonnie Redan. Gage was shown for six months in Canada last year, finishing the year as the number two Canadian Silky. He came within 43 points of taking the number one spot. He is being shown again

Am Ch. Tawny Mist
Shalee Del Rio: Rio is a
multiple Group and Best
in Show winner for both
Best Puppy and Best
Bred by Exhibitor at
international all-breed
Kennel Club shows. She
is also a multiple Group-
placer in the US.

Booth Photography.

this year in Canada and is currently tied as number one. He has taken numerous Group firsts during both 1995 and 1996. He has also produced some beautiful puppies for his co-owner, Diane Miller from Niagara-on-the-Lake, Ontario, Canada. Gage is also co-owned by Donna Renton and Shauna Jones and he will return to the US in 1997.

Rio has multiple Best Puppy in Show awards. She took three consecutive Best Puppy in Show wins and two consecutive Best Bred by Puppy in Show wins at IABKC shows. She was reserve Winners Bitch at the 1995 National Specialty and is a multiple Group placing Silky. She is owned by Steve and Donna Renton. Bonnie, and her litter brother, Roy, have both made a nice showing in the ring. Bonnie finished her US Championship by the time she was nine months old. She lives with her owner, Renee Daniels, in Jacksonville, Fl. Roy also finished his Championship easily by taking Best of Breed wins over adult Champions. Roy is owned by Shauna. Once he has had time to mature, she plans to continue to show him as a Special. She has recently used him at stud and he has produced some nice puppies. Shauna is trying hard to develop a quality breeding program and is currently having some excellent results.

ANOVA
MICHAEL AND SUELLEN SHANKER
Manassas, Virginia.

The Shankers obtained their first Silky for show in 1980 from Gene and Paula Huff of Chrisbonli's Silkies. Ch. Chrisbonli's Casey Luv'n easily earned her Championship and was Best of Opposite Sex in Sweepstakes at the 1981 National Specialty. Casey was a multiple Group placing Silky, producer of

Am. Ch. Anova's Prime Time (Am. Ch. Lucknow Local Talent – Am. Ch. Silwynd's Waltzing Matilda: Best in Sweepstakes, Winners Dog and Best of Winners 1996 National Specialty.

Booth Photography.

two Champions and grandam of 17 Champions. One of Casey's grand get, Ch. Anova's Wyncrest Traveler, was top in the National Specialty for 1989, 1990 and 1991. He has a total of 14 Championship titles to his credit and was Best of Breed at the World Dog Show in Copenhagen, Denmark in 1989 and Best of Breed at the prestigious Westminster Kennel Club show held in New York, NY, every February. Traveler also received Awards of Merit at the 1990, 1991 and 1992 National Specialties. Traveler is owned by Jean Schmidt from Wisconsin.

Two of Casey's other grand get, Ch. Anova's Kash N Karry and Ch. Alcamar-N-Blu-Star's Jasmine, both have done well in the show ring. Kash N Karry was a top US Special during 1989. Along the way to

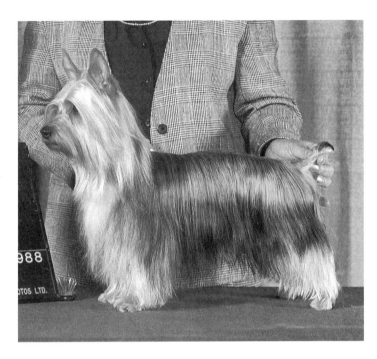

Am. Ch. Anova's Wyncrest Traveler: American, Canadian, Bahamian, Costa Rican, Chilean, Colombian, Guatemalan, Mexican, States, Las Americas, South American, FCI Intl, Copenhagen (both winter and World) Championships.

Photo: Mikron.

Jasmine's Championship she was Winners Bitch and Best of Winners at the 1993 National Specialty. Jasmine was bred by Anne and Nelson Wright and is owned by Carol Marshall. In 1991 the Shankers obtained an addition to their breeding program. They purchased Ch. Silwynd's Waltzing Matilda, ROM, known as Tillie, from Bill and Rita Dawson. During her show career, Tillie was a Group placer. She has produced a total of five Champions to date. Her daughter, Ch. Anova's Wyndsome Carolina, was the 1994 Best in Sweepstakes winner. Her son, Ch. Anova's Prime Time, was Best in Sweepstakes, Winners Dog and Best of Winners at the 1996 National Specialty. While the Shankers only breed on a limited basis, it's obvious they have been successful with their breeding program.

OBEDIENCE BREEDERS AND/OR EXHIBITORS

KHARA
Linda Hart
Littleton, Colorado.

Originally initiated into the world of pure-bred dogs with Dobermanns, Linda Hart found Silkies to be just as intelligent and quick to learn as large breeds. She now shows her Silkies in Obedience and in Conformation. Her first show and Obedience prospect, Tru Blu Bei Under My Spell, came to her at just eight weeks of age. She went from being a vivacious little puppy to become the top winning Obedience Silky in the history of the breed. Bei was shown in both Obedience and Conformation simultaneously until she earned her Championship. She knew that a change of collars indicated which ring she was competing in and she would perform flawlessly for each.

She competed in Obedience for a total of eight years, obtaining her Companion Dog (CD), Companion Dog Excellent (CDX) and Utility Dog (UD) titles. While competing she obtained four all-breed High in Trial wins, and two all-breed High Combined awards. She was also awarded the Silky Terrier Club's top Obedience honor, the Stroud Mandy Fowler Award, six out of eight years. Bei also participated in Obedience and training demonstrations throughout her career and during retirement, at school and in public events. She has even competed at practice terrier "go-to-ground" events. All of these events have been fun for Bei and show the versatility and capability of the breed. At thirteen years of age Bei is still healthy and active. She lets the other Silkies of the household know she's still "top dog". As well as being an exhibitor, Linda Hart is

also a breeder who has produced some find Silkies. She continues to breed on a limited basis, striving to produce the "perfect Silky' for both temperament and conformation.

DOLLIE FOLAND
Indianapolis, Indiana.

Dollie Foland's primary interest in the breed is for Obedience. Her Obedience Silky, Sun Dances Rhythm n'Blue, UDX, known as Rocky, has made quite a name for himself in the show ring. He has a number of High in Trial and High Combined wins to his credit, including his HIT at the 1990 National Specialty. He has also been the number one US Obedience Silky for several years. Rocky is the only Silky with a Dog World title and he was ranked 9th at the Dog World trials. He was the first US Silky to obtain his UDX title. He has taught Dollie, and her husband Raymond, patience and perseverance. He sleeps with them at night and spends the rest of his day

Am. Ch. Shalee's Peppermint Stick CD, CGC: 1996 National Specialty, High in Trial.

Booth Photography.

157

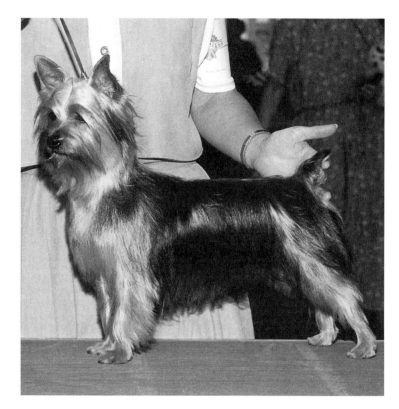

Am. Ch. Deja's Kissed by Tawny Mist: Shown by her owner, Mary Ellen Vickery.

Photo: Downey.

by their side. Rocky also has the distinction of being cast as Toto in the play *The Wizard of Oz.*

Dollie's secrets to success in the Obedience ring are:

1) make your dog think it's his idea.

2) stay away from your dog for a couple of hours before ring time – it makes him happier to work for you.

3) introduce new exercises with food – after he learns the exercise, make up a treat pot and reward your dog at the end of the exercise.

4) use an antenna with a clip taped to the end to give your dog treats – it really saves your back!

5) start your dog on "standing" on the table – have many people go over him, then reward him.

6) train your puppy the command Come early – keep a pocket full of treats then call your puppy to you several times a day – he'll keep coming back for more!

*A*PPENDIX

UK INFORMATION
To obtain a complete copy of the current
official Breed Standard write to:
The English Kennel Club,
1-5 Clarges Street, Piccadilly,
London, W1Y 8AB.

For more information apply to:
Miss A. Marshall,
Marshdae, Whiteholme Road,
Thornton Cleveleys, Blackpool,
Lancashire, FY5 3HX.

US INFORMATION
To obtain a complete copy of the current
official Breed Standard write to:
The American Kennel Club,
51 Madison Avenue,
New York,
NY 10010.

For more information apply to:
The Silky Terrier Club of America Inc.
(STCA),
PO Box 1132,
Alameda,
California 94501.

You may also write to the STCA and/or

the breed clubs listed below for more
information about Silky Terriers as well as
current breeder lists or membership
applications:
Gulf Coast Silky Terrier Club
13335 Little Ranch Road
Cypress, TX. 77429.

City of Angels Silky Terrier Club,
5766 Saturn Ct.
San Barnardina, CA. 92407.

Chesapeake Silky Terrier Club,
5000 Tall Oaks Drive
Blacksburg, VA. 24060.

Maple Leaf Silky Terrier Club,
Box 57 Vibank, SK, SOG 4YO, Canada.

AUSTRALIA
To obtain a complete copy of the current
official Breed Standard write to:
Australian National Kennel Council
PO Box 285,
Red Hill South,
Victoria 3937,
Australia.